LIVING IN
CONSCIOUS HARMONY

LIVING IN CONSCIOUS HARMONY

A Spiritual Guide to Being in the Now

SULLINS STUART, M.A.

To Sarah, Tristan, and Emily

You don't have a soul. You are a soul. You have a body.

— C.S. Lewis

Compared to what we ought to be, we are half awake.

— William James

Three things cannot be long hidden: the sun, the moon, and the truth.

— The Buddha

CONTENTS

Preface   XIII

PART I: THE FUNDAMENTALS TO BEING IN THE NOW

WE ARE ONE SOUL   3

THE FOUR STATES OF CONSCIOUSNESS   7

FIVE WAYS TO LIVE IN THE NOW   17

KNOWLEDGE, UNDERSTANDING & BEING   27

THE POWER OF THOUGHT   33

THE BENEFITS TO LIVING IN CONSCIOUS HARMONY   39

PART II: THE ART OF LIVING IN CONSCIOUS HARMONY

THE PRESENT AWAITS YOU   45

THE KEY TO HAPPINESS   49

THE BIG FLOOD   53

MASTER YOUR FATE   57

REALIZE YOUR FULL POTENTIAL   59

LETTING GO OF SUFFERING   67

THE SECOND COMING   71

THE LAW OF RECURRENCE   75

BEING PRESENT WITH CHILDREN — 81

TRANSFORMING REAL SUFFERING — 83

BE HERE NOW — 87

CREATIVITY & DIVINE INSPIRATION — 89

USE THE PRESENT TO HEAL THE PAST — 93

A SPIRITUAL PERSPECTIVE ON DEATH — 97

HEAVEN AND HELL — 101

YOUR BEING ATTRACTS YOUR LIFE — 103

UNLEASH YOUR SOUL — 107

ENVELOPING OTHERS WITH DIVINE LOVE — 111

THE EYE OF THE STORM — 115

LIVING AUTHENTICALLY — 117

FEAR — 121

GENERATIONAL RECURRENCE — 123

RELEASE YOUR INNER BUDDHA — 127

GET IN SPIRITUAL SHAPE — 131

NATURE IS FOOD FOR THE SOUL — 135

PART III: QUESTION AND ANSWER

A SPIRITUAL CRISIS EXISTS — 139

THE NATURE OF SPIRITUAL WORK — 145

SPIRITUAL AWAKENING — 149

BEING PRESENT — 153

FORGIVENESS & COMPASSION — 161

DEALING WITH REGRET — 165

NOT EXPRESSING NEGATIVE EMOTIONS — 167

DEALING WITH FEAR   169

CONSCIOUS ART   171

CHANGING ANOTHER'S CONSCIOUSNESS   173

REINCARNATION   177

EPILOGUE

A MESSAGE OF THANKS   179

ABOUT THE AUTHOR   183

PREFACE

My aim in writing this book is to assist you in living in *conscious harmony with God*, the Infinite Spirit and Power of the Universe. The key principle to living in conscious harmony is to be in the Present, the eternal Now.

Living in conscious harmony is a mystical experience revealing a world of infinite possibilities. In the Now you enter a higher state of consciousness and become aware of your true nature as a spiritual Being. You see God everywhere and in everything, and you realize the divine Truth—*all is one with God, all is God*. Possessing the higher knowledge and understanding that only God is real, only God exists, you become a God-realized soul. As a God-realized soul, you are no longer bound by the limitations of the physical body or the world of forms.

The ego, being identified with the body and

attached to the material world, prevents you from living in the Present. It takes knowledge, under-standing, desire, and effort to escape the prison of the ego.

It is important to make the effort to live in the Now, for each moment you spend in the Present will remind you of a forgotten truth — you are not the body or mind, but the loving, radiant, divine energy that is God. *In the Present you fulfill your destiny as a spiritual Being.*

I do not subscribe to any one religion. I believe the divine Truth can be found in Buddhism, Taoism, Christianity, Islam, Sikhism, Hinduism, and Judaism, if not all the major religions of the world.

However, having been born and raised in the United States where Christianity is the dominant religion, many of my essays will reference Jesus or God. It is not my intention, nor my role, to lead anyone to Christianity, nor do I endorse Christianity over Buddhism, or any other religion. Christianity just so happens to be the religion of my country of origin, and most likely, the religion of many of my readers.

More importantly, my sincere desire for you, the

reader, is to assist you in awakening your soul, no matter your spiritual or religious preference. And remember, *the path you take towards spiritual awakening is not what is important; that you arrive at your destination is what matters most.*

Peace and Blessings,

Sullins Stuart

Austin, Texas

December 5, 2011

PART I

THE FUNDAMENTALS TO BEING IN THE NOW

Everyone thinks of changing the world, but no one thinks of changing himself.

— Leo Tolstoy

WE ARE ONE SOUL

We live in succession, in division, in parts, in particles. Meantime within man is the soul of the whole; the wise silence; the universal beauty, to which every part and particle is equally related; the eternal ONE...We see the world piece by piece as the sun, the moon, the animal, the tree; but the whole, of which these are the shining parts, is the soul.

— Ralph Waldo Emerson

There is but one soul, a universal soul or over-soul, of which you are a part. The source of this universal soul is the Infinite Spirit and Creator of all that exists. It is called God, Allah, Yahweh, Brahman, Krishna — the name is irrelevant. *It* is beyond labels and definitions. However, man often does not see it this way. We forget we are souls and identify with our bodies, our thoughts, opinions, and beliefs. Therefore, we cannot help but see how different we are from our Creator and one another.

Suppose I ask, "Who are you?"

Your response will probably include your name, age, gender, race, marital status, religion, level of education, whether or not you have children, where you live, and your occupation. These characteristics define you physically, emotionally, intellectually, and instinctively, and combined with the ego, dictate how you view and interpret events occurring in and around your world.

The ego creates your identity as a human, and it is the ego that views itself as being separate from others. Your identification with your body and mind tells you that no two people are alike. No one has the exact same experiences as you. No one sees the world exactly as you.

Our fixation with whom and what we are, and who and what we are not, transcends our individual identities. We gravitate towards like-minded people and begin to identify ourselves by social class, church or religious affiliation, neighborhood, city, and country. Hence, what distinguishes you from me, your groups from my groups, and your country from my country, becomes the source of all selfishness, greed, lust, crime, suffering, prejudice, conflict, and destruction in the world.

The ego creates a veil of ignorance, a false sense of identity, which shields us from our true nature as souls. The more we identify with our thoughts, opinions, and physical characteristics, the further we remove ourselves from the Divine. As a result, *we forget we are souls. We forget our connection to something higher than ourselves. We forget all are one.*

Pretend you are at the beach. Imagine the ocean is the Infinite Spirit. You have in your hand a cup that you submerge and fill with ocean water. Is the water in the cup different from the ocean water from which it was removed? Will it have a different energy, or a different molecular makeup? Will it differ in any way? No, it will be identical. However, the water in the cup *has been separated from its source.* Only in isolation does the part appear to be different from the whole. The same is true for you. Your soul is identical to the universal soul from which you have become separated. There is no difference. Herein, lies your spiritual objective: *you are here to awaken your soul and return to the Source.*

In order for your soul to return to the Source, you must always strive to live in the Present, for it is in the Present that your soul escapes the prison of the ego, awakens, and reconnects with the Divine.

THE FOUR STATES OF CONSCIOUSNESS

Our normal waking consciousness, rational consciousness as we call it, is but one special type of consciousness, whilst all about it, parted from it by the flimsiest of screens, there lie potential forms of consciousness entirely different. We may go through life without suspecting their existence, but apply the requisite stimulus, and at a touch they are there in their completeness, definite types of mentality which probably somewhere have their field of application and adaptation. No account of the universe in its totality can be final which leaves these other forms of consciousness quite disregarded.

— William James

P. D. Ouspensky discusses in detail the four states of consciousness in his book *The Psychology of Man's Possible Evolution*. I will mention them briefly. They are *sleep* (first state), *waking sleep* (second state), *self-consciousness* (third state), and *objective consciousness* (fourth state). Each state, or level, is distinct and there is a significant difference in the amount of awareness and consciousness associated with each one. As you move from first to second to third to fourth state you experience an increase in consciousness.

The first and second states are lower levels of consciousness pertaining to the body and mind. You spend almost your entire life in the first and second states.

The third and fourth states are higher levels of consciousness pertaining to the soul and spirit. These two states are *mystical states of being* and have been written about for hundreds and thousands of years by saints, prophets, spiritual teachers, and other enlightened men and women.

The First State of Consciousness

The first state of consciousness is the lowest level of awareness and consciousness in which you exist. It is known as *sleep*. This is the state you enter when you go to bed. A typical person will spend approximately a third of his life in this state of suspended consciousness and limited awareness.

The Second State of Consciousness

You enter the second state of consciousness, *waking sleep*, when you awaken from the first state. On average, a person will spend approximately two-thirds of their life in this state. It is known as "waking sleep" because you are physically awake, *but you are not present*. You are minimally conscious, meaning you are cognizant of your existence but your mind is preoccupied with other things. Just as airplane pilots can engage the autopilot function in their aircraft, you unknowingly experience a great deal of your life in a state of consciousness similar to being on autopilot.

Have you ever driven somewhere and wondered how you arrived at your destination because you were not paying attention to your driving? Have you ever walked into a room of your home only to forget what it was you were seeking? Have you ever been reading a book, arrived at the bottom of a page, and realized you don't remember what you just read? Do you have to think about how to ride a bike? Button a shirt? Tie your shoes? All of these acts become automatic once you have performed them repeatedly. As a result, you can do numerous tasks while you are actually thinking of something else. This is how you live most of your life—you go through the motions of living while your mind is focused on other things.

The Third State of Consciousness

You experience the third state of consciousness when you make the effort to be in the Present. This state is called *self-consciousness* or *self-awareness* because *you intentionally make the effort to observe yourself.* It is a higher state of consciousness, much higher than your normal, everyday existence in the second state. In addition, it is in the third state that you experience *spiritual awakening – the awakening of your soul.*

Spiritual awakening is often called a *re-birth.* When your soul awakens you experience an elevated level of consciousness, awareness, and Being. You realize you are not the body or ego, but an immortal soul. If you live most of your life in this higher state of consciousness, you have been re-born because you have dropped the ego, and allowed your soul to direct and dominate your existence.

In the second state of consciousness the ego is the driving force behind your thoughts and actions. With the ego in charge, you view yourself and your world *subjectively*. In the third state of consciousness you engage your soul and view yourself *objectively*. To experience the third state can be life-changing because once you begin to observe yourself, you realize you actually live most of your life in waking sleep, a state of limited consciousness and minimal awareness.

The ego is king in the second state of con-sciousness, and the king is constantly threatened of you living in the Now because in the third state of consciousness, the ego disappears. In the Now, you observe the ego for what it really is—nothing but an illusion, and the source of all desire, pain, and suffering.

Observing yourself is not innate. Do you recall the things I mentioned earlier that you do automatically?

As an experiment, *try observing yourself doing those activities.* Intentionally observe yourself driving a car. Note the numerous functions that must be performed. Where are your hands? How are you gripping the steering wheel? Are your shoulders and back tense or relaxed? How are you seated? Where are your feet? How often do you check the mirrors for other cars? How much pressure do you exert on the gas and the brake pedals. Become consciously aware of all the things that simultaneously occur in order for you to drive a car.

Or, observe yourself writing a check, or creating a to-do list. Become aware of the pen or pencil in your hand. Are you holding it loosely or tightly? Which fingers do you use when you are writing? Do you press hard against the paper? Note how you make each individual letter of each word. Do you write in print, cursive, or a mixture of both? How far apart do you space your letters? As an adult, you don't have to think about how to draw each letter of the alphabet; it has long been automatic. But, slow down and intentionally note all the functions that are required for you to write just one letter, one word, one sentence. You may find yourself in amazement of the process.

People tell me that observing yourself feels like an out of body experience. *When you observe yourself, you are present and outside of time.* You may feel like you are out of your body because you realize *you are not the body,* but something much higher *that observes the body.*

The third level of consciousness has multitudes of levels within it. If you are just starting to make the effort to be in the Now, you will probably discover your moments of presence are short-lived and infrequent. Don't despair. In time, they will increase in duration, frequency, and intensity, but not without practice. So, observe, observe, observe.

The Fourth State of Consciousness

The fourth state, and highest level of consciousness, is *objective consciousness* or *spiritual enlightenment.* In the third state of consciousness you engage the soul and become objective to yourself. In the fourth state *you engage the spirit and become objective to the world.* You see everything in its true form, as distinct frequencies and vibrations of energy. There are multitudes of layers within this state of consciousness, too.

While the fourth state of consciousness is within reach of everyone, achieving it and remaining there is rare. Typically, to enter into this realm of existence requires having lived many years in a state of continual presence. Throughout history individuals have spiritually awakened, but far fewer have actually become enlightened. Jesus, Buddha, Mohammad, Moses, and Lao Tzu are a few who reached the fourth state of consciousness in their lifetime.

It is important to have a working knowledge of the four states of consciousness, primarily the second and third states. When you experience the third state, you verify the second state is nothing more than the ego identified with itself. All problems, both personal and global, are the result of individuals living in the second state of consciousness, where their lives are dictated by the ego.

Your spiritual objective is to live as much of

your life as you can in the third state of consciousness — the eternal Now.

FIVE WAYS TO LIVE IN THE NOW

Remember then: there is only one time that is important—Now! It is the most important time because it is the only time when we have any power.

— Leo Tolstoy

I have found many spiritual and philosophical books discuss the importance of being in the Here and Now, yet very few mention how to do it. When discussing the idea of living in conscious harmony and being in the Present, often the first question I am asked is, "I understand being in the moment, but I'm not sure how to do it, or if I'm doing it correctly?" I have good news and bad news. The good news…I'm going to tell you how to live in the Present. The bad news…with knowledge comes responsibility. You will no longer be able to say you do not know how to be present which means you will be responsible for whether or not you are making the effort to live in the Now.

I'm going to discuss five ways in which you can live in the Now: *Grace, Shocks, Divided Attention, Intentional Awareness, and Assistance from a Spiritual Teacher.*

Grace

The first way to be in the Present is through *grace*. With grace, the eternal Now finds you and envelopes you with its radiant, peaceful, loving energy. In other words, you suddenly find yourself living in the Present without having made any effort. This can occur anytime, anywhere.

I have encountered grace under a multitude of circumstances: while driving, reading, jogging, in a theatre, listening to music, watching a sunset, gardening, et cetera. You never know when grace will occur. However, you can put yourself in circumstances that may increase your chances of receiving it. I have found that I often encounter grace when I'm with nature.

Nature has the inherent ability to bring you into the moment. Have you ever witnessed a beautiful, scenic environment and suddenly felt totally at one with nature? So much so, your mind was emptied of all thought and you felt an overwhelming sense of peacefulness? Such is the power of nature.

When grace occurs, presence descends upon you like a gentle wave. You may find you are able to remain present and ride the wave for just a few seconds or maybe several minutes. Either way, ride the wave of presence as long as it lasts, then give thanks to the Infinite Spirit for bestowing grace upon you. *These moments are a gift from Above.*

Shocks

The second way to be in the Present is via a *shock*. As with grace, shocks bring you into the moment. A shock occurs when you experience something outside of your ordinary routine or daily life. Shocks can be good, like the birth of your child or your wedding day, or not so good, such as being involved in a car accident or experiencing the death of a friend or family member. Any number of circumstances can shock you into the Present. Typically, the greater the shock the longer you remain in the Now.

Have you ever been driving and something catches your attention and you take your eyes off the road just for a split second? Suddenly, you realize the car in front of you has stopped, forcing you to slam on the brakes to avoid rear-ending it. You quickly find yourself thrust into the moment. Usually, this moment of presence doesn't last very long, and fades away as you resume driving.

On the other hand, let's say you have recently experienced a large shock, such as the death of a dear friend. Shocks such as these will have a far greater impact upon you. Large shocks can bring you into the Present for several days or longer.

Often, the magnitude of large shocks will cause an individual to re-evaluate their life, their marriage, their job, and so on. Re-evaluating life on this scale sometimes will lead an individual to make drastic changes because death reminds us of the brevity of life. However, a word of caution is in order. In the midst of experiencing a large shock, either the soul or the ego will be the main force in determining your response. If it is the ego, watch out. The choices it makes can be severe and irreparable.

The ego, by its very nature, fears its own demise. The death of someone close to you re-inforces this fear. In this situation your ego may convince you to act destructively and have an affair, quit your job, spend money lavishly on things you can't afford, or indulge in reckless behavior. The ego will justify this behavior stating, "Life is short. Live it to the fullest!"

However, the proper way to utilize a large shock is to use it as food for the soul. Life is short and you should live it to the fullest, but *you can do this by making sure you actually experience each day.* Vow today to be the best at whatever you do, whether it is being a spouse, a parent, a friend, a boss, or employee. Vow to not judge others, be envious, jealous, or to express negativity. Vow to be grateful and thankful for today, for today is all you really have. Live, so that at the end of today you can look in the mirror and have no regrets. This is how you transform a large shock into food for the soul.

As with small shocks, the state of presence you experience from a large shock diminishes with time. You then find yourself absorbed in your normal routines, reverting to previous behaviors and patterns of thought, until another shock comes along to bring you into the Present.

Divided Attention

The third way to be in the Now is through a technique called *divided attention*. Unlike grace and shocks, divided attention requires that you make the effort to be in the Present. Divided attention is a process in which you split your attention between two objects or tasks.

For example, locate an object such as a candle, plant, vase, anything in your immediate environment upon which you can place your visual attention. With your attention firmly placed on the chosen object, you are going to introduce a second object to focus upon, such as repeating a word or phrase. Begin to repeat, "I am in the Here and Now." The goal is to maintain your visual attention while also putting your attention on your speech. If you find that your mind wanders, stop and start over.

When you successfully divide your attention, without your mind wandering, *attempt to become aware of what is observing you as you perform this activity.* Your mind is focused visually and vocally, but something else is doing the observing—*your soul.* When you are able to observe yourself dividing your attention, you will notice your mind becomes still. You are in the Present…welcome to the Now!

Divided attention is not a new concept. The Christian Mystics incorporated divided attention into prayer in their efforts to seek union with God. They possessed the knowledge and understanding that divided attention created an opportunity for the soul to manifest.

With practice you will be able to divide your attention anytime, anywhere. If possible, try it right now. Sit upright either in a chair or on the floor. Place your hands, palms up, in your lap. Note how your hands are placed, how each individual finger looks, pay attention to the lines, calluses, and veins.

As you maintain your attention on your hands, slowly and with intention, become aware of your breathing, noting each breath as it goes in and out. If your mind wanders, stop and start over.

At the precise moment you experience detachment and timelessness, you will have entered the third state of consciousness. In this moment, you will be present; you will be living in the Now. Remember, this takes practice. In time, you will be able to divide your attention with ease.

(To view a video demonstration of Dividing Your Attention visit www.livinginconsciousharmony.com and click on the Videos tab.)

Intentional Awareness

The fourth way to be in the Now, *intentional awareness*, is a variation of divided attention. Using this technique, you bring intention and awareness to whatever task you are currently performing. In other words, whatever you are doing, *really do it*. Rarely do we do anything with our full attention because our minds are usually preoccupied with other things.

Take a moment to think about all the tasks that

you do throughout a normal day. Would you say that most of those things were accomplished while you were thinking of or preoccupied with something else? You had to give all of these tasks a lot of thought when you were learning how to do them the first time, but now they are performed automatically, without requiring any thought. Consider this…if you were to perform every single task you undertook in a day with intention and awareness, at the end of the day you would be exhausted because you are not accustomed to doing things with all your Being.

For example, the next time you drink a beverage, note the following: How are you holding the cup, loosely or tightly? How does it feel in your hands? Is the rim smooth or rough? Is the beverage hot or cold? What does the cup feel like when pressed against your lips? When the liquid hits your tongue, what sensations occur in your mouth? Become acutely aware of all the physical processes that occur just for you to swallow one sip. Hundreds of mental and physical processes take place just for you to lift the cup and take a drink.

Your goal is *to do everything with awareness,*

intention, and purpose. It may seem impossible at first, but with practice it gets easier. Furthermore, it will change your life. You will begin to hear more, see more, feel more, and experience more. It will enrich your relationships. And, you will feel more alive because you will be more alive—you will be living in the Now.

Assistance from a Spiritual Teacher

The fifth way to be in the Now does not happen often; it is quite rare. It occurs when someone, such as a spiritual teacher, possesses the ability to pull you into the Now. I don't believe there are many on the planet with this ability, but these individuals do exist. I know because my teacher was one of them.

As you practice living in the Present, you will discover there are many facets to it. Your moments of presence will differ in duration and intensity. However, it is not enough to have knowledge about being present, you must take action. Practice being present always and everywhere!

KNOWLEDGE, UNDERSTANDING & BEING

A little knowledge that acts is worth infinitely more than much knowledge that is idle.

— Khalil Gibran

I hear, I know. I see, I remember. I do, I understand.

—Confucius

There are several ways to overcome the power of the ego and engage the soul. Some practice yoga or meditate, some use divided attention. Regardless the method you use, it will require that you have *knowledge, understanding, and being.*

To have *knowledge* is to know the facts or

information on a specific subject. *Understanding* occurs when you thoroughly comprehend the knowledge or facts. You attain *being* when you successfully apply the knowledge and understanding of the given subject or task.

For example, I have no being in winemaking. However, I can go to a bookstore or library and check out numerous books on how to become a winemaker. I can study the various types of grapes, the specific climates required for their cultivation, and how to protect them against pests and disease. I can learn about the crush, fermenting the grapes, as well as, the advantages and disadvantages of using oak barrels. In fact, with a lot of study, I can gain a vast amount of knowledge about winemaking without ever growing a single grape. But, that is all I would possess — knowledge.

In order for me to gain *understanding* in the art of winemaking, I would need to *apply my knowledge.* This would probably entail traveling to California, Oregon, or Washington, and working at a winery. True understanding of any subject requires the direct application of the knowledge gained, usually under the tutelage of a teacher or master. With understanding, you learn the many subtle nuances regarding a subject or task that knowledge alone cannot provide.

Once you begin to apply your understanding of a subject, you gain *being* in that area. If being continues to grow you become a master or teacher. Continuing with my example, as I attain *being* in winemaking, I would eventually be qualified to manage a winery, or possibly purchase acreage and vines, and start a winery of my own. However, the effort to attain being does not stop once it has been achieved. It is an ongoing, organic process because knowledge and understanding changes and grows with an increase in one's being. If you don't allow for new knowledge and new understanding to occur, over time your being will start to diminish.

How does this apply to your spiritual growth and awakening?

It is important that you find a valid spiritual teaching that you can practice, or a spiritual teacher to guide you in matters pertaining to the soul. It is possible to awaken on your own, but it is rare.

Remember, knowledge and being must grow in tandem. As your being increases, you are able to absorb more knowledge. New knowledge creates the opportunity for more growth in being. It is a reciprocal process—growth in one allows for growth in the other, and vice versa. However, you must make the effort to take in more knowledge, and you must make the effort to grow in being. It doesn't happen automatically. Understanding occurs when both knowledge and being are increasing simultaneously. However, for understanding to grow, you must have growth in being. Growth in knowledge alone does not allow for an increase in understanding.

To spiritually evolve, knowledge and being should grow in harmony with one another. It is easy for knowledge or being to grow and the other to lag behind or remain stagnant. It takes effort to make sure they grow parallel to one another. If they grow at disproportional rates or at the expense of the other for too long, your spiritual evolution will eventually come to a stop. G. I. Gurdjieff, a Greek-Armenian spiritual teacher and mystic, referred to individuals whose spiritual being or spiritual knowledge outweighed the other as *stupid saints* and *weak yogis.*

A stupid saint is someone whose spiritual being is greater than the amount of spiritual knowledge he possesses. This person will have the ability to lead a spiritual life, but their lack of real spiritual knowledge and understanding prevents them from accomplishing anything of true spiritual value. For example, a stupid saint might have a lot of being in practicing meditation several times a day, but lack the knowledge or understanding to fully reap its spiritual benefits. Or, they may be experienced at the non-expression of negative emotions, but not know or realize how to transform negative emotions into presence or to utilize it for the growth of their soul.

A weak yogi is someone whose spiritual knowledge is far greater than their level of spiritual being. In other words, it is an individual who knows a great deal of information, but doesn't know what to do with it. Spiritually speaking, someone could study all the great religions and spiritual teachers, but not have a real understanding of any of them. Their spiritual knowledge may be impressive, but if they lack the ability to understand and act on their knowledge, then it is virtually useless information.

To reiterate, knowledge and being should increase at the same time. If you pay attention to one at the expense of the other, your spiritual growth will eventually become skewed and stop. Furthermore, spiritual understanding increases when knowledge and being grow in unison. Understanding does not occur solely with an increase in knowledge.

Your spiritual growth is a lifelong process. Through aim and effort, you can increase your spiritual knowledge and spiritual being. If you work on both at the same time, you will increase your spiritual understanding too, and your spiritual growth and evolution will proceed in a healthy, unified manner.

THE POWER OF THOUGHT

Belief creates the actual fact.

— William James

The subconscious mind will translate into reality a thought driven by fear just as readily as it will translate into reality a thought driven by courage or faith.

— Napoleon Hill

You are what you think you are. Your thoughts form the very foundation for everything in your life. Your thoughts influence your moods, your feelings, and your opinions. How you choose to respond to your thoughts determines your physical, mental, and emotional reality each day.

Thoughts contain energy. Every thought your

brain produces travels unseen through space, vibrating at a specific frequency, just like radio and television waves. When your thoughts are combined with emotion or intention, they become more powerful. Strongly held beliefs and faith are capable of bringing calm and peace of mind during difficult times, just as thoughts of anger or intense rage can lead to very destructive behavior.

Your thoughts affect every cell of your body. Psychologists and medical researchers have long known about the power of thought due to the placebo effect—a common phenomenon in which patients recover from ailments after being administered an inactive substance. In fact, *the mere suggestion of having received treatment* has been shown to have a significant effect in the recovery of one out of three individuals. Furthermore, researchers have actually recorded brain activity in response to placebos, which further verifies the strong connection and relationship between mind and body.

If you want a life of infinite peace, love, and joy, you must believe you are capable and worthy of it. In the eternal Present *anything is possible.* In the Present, you rise above the barriers and limitations imposed by the ego and the world of forms. To have the life you desire and deserve, first, you must live in the Now, and second, *you must believe it is possible, you must have faith.*

Suppose you are a highly, self-critical person. You often think, "I'm not as smart as others. I'm not as attractive as others. I don't have what it takes to succeed. I'll never have enough money," and so on. You will never be more than you currently are because you don't believe it's possible.

You attract into your life what you think and believe on a daily basis. It is very simple—it's the *Law of Attraction.* If you think you aren't good enough, you never will be. If you think you aren't smart enough, you never will be. What you think and believe about yourself and your abilities becomes a self-fulfilling prophecy.

Conversely, suppose you are a positive, always happy individual who appears to lead a charmed life. You succeed at everything you attempt. Things always go your way. You see the positive in situations and people. Why wouldn't you have a charmed life? You think that life is great, and it is. You believe you can do anything you set your mind to, and you do. By the very nature of your positive thoughts, you attract success and joy into your life. Yet, positive thinking will only get you so far.

In order to have a life in conscious harmony with the Infinite Spirit, a life in which all things are possible, you must be present and engage your soul — *the God that exists within you*. There is nothing more powerful than the ability to be present accompanied by faith. In the Now, all limitations disappear. In faith, lies the expectation of fulfillment. *Have faith in the power of the Now.*

If you are unhappy or unfulfilled, I encourage you to look at the thoughts you have throughout your day. You may discover your thoughts are predominantly negative and self-critical. If so, it is time to make a change in your thought process. Negative thinking produces negative behavior. Positive thinking produces positive behavior. Begin to think and believe you are a vibrant, creative, beautiful, loving person, and life is truly wonderful, and in time you will feel and act as though you are a vibrant, creative, beautiful, loving person, whose life is wonderful.

Gandhi wisely stated, *"Be the change you wish to see in the world."* It really is quite simple. Change starts with you. More specifically, *change starts with changing your thoughts.* And, if you question your ability to manifest this change, remember this…*you are not the mind or the body. You are a beautiful, immortal soul born of God. You can transform yourself in the eternal Present through the intentional projection of thoughts born of divine Love accompanied by the belief that anything is possible.*

THE BENEFITS TO LIVING IN CONSCIOUS HARMONY

Rejoice in the things that are present; all else is beyond thee.

— Michel de Montaigne

When you live in conscious harmony…

…you engage your soul.

…you awaken.

…you experience a deep awareness of yourself and your environment.

…you have no judgment.

…you possess unconditional love for all that exists.

…you understand you are pure energy.

…all is revealed.

…you recognize there are unseen laws that govern man and the universe.

…your mind is still, void of thought.

…you see everything in its true form, just as God intended.

…you realize you are connected to everything that exists.

…you experience timelessness.

…you recognize there are no absolutes; everything just *is*.

…you understand there are no accidents; everything happens for a reason.

…fear and imagination are replaced with unconditional love and truth.

…you realize you are an immortal soul encased in a mortal body.

…you realize through unconditional love anything is possible.

…you understand why Jesus said, "Love your enemies."

…you gain divine wisdom.

…you see tremendous healing could occur on Earth if more people made an effort to live in conscious harmony.

...you see everything as being perfect and beautiful.

...you realize thoughts contain energy and are very powerful.

...you understand that each day you choose to be in heaven or hell.

...you realize your soul and the soul of Jesus are the same soul.

...you understand death is nothing to fear because the soul does not die.

...you observe having a thought and not voicing it, is no different from speaking it aloud.

...you realize our planet is sacred, and we must show it love and respect.

...you gain the knowledge that you possess the ability to direct loving, healing energy to others near and far, and it will affect them.

...you observe your ego has no desire to live in the Present or to acknowledge the existence of your soul.

...you realize you have lived many lifetimes and experienced being many different life forms, but always with the same soul.

…you realize you must make every effort to live in the Present all the time.

…you realize when you are living in the Present, you must make every effort to remain in the Present.

PART II

THE ART OF LIVING IN CONSCIOUS HARMONY

The soul is the bridge connecting you to God.

— Sullins Stuart

THE PRESENT AWAITS YOU

To be a living being is not the ultimate state; there is something beyond much more wonderful, which is neither being nor non-being, neither living nor not living. It is a state of pure awareness, beyond the limitations of space and time.

— Sri Nisargadatta Maharaj

Confine yourself to the present.

— Marcus Aurelius

The Present *is* and awaits you to engage it. The Present is infinite and timeless; hence, it is known as the *eternal Now*. The Present is beyond duality, beyond judgment. *It is Truth*. If you are in the Present, you are experiencing a higher state of consciousness, a higher state of awareness. If you want to know your true nature and the truth regarding your existence, the truth regarding the existence of everything, *be present*. All other moments are an illusion. If you are not in the Present, you are absorbed in thoughts keeping you in the past or the future. And if you are absorbed in the past or future, you are not truly living. *Life is only real in the present moment — the Here and Now.*

So, why aren't you naturally in the present moment? Because the ego is very powerful. It protects itself by preventing you from living in the Now, and convincing you all your thoughts, opinions, and actions are valid and real. However, enter into a state of presence, and the ego loses its power and disappears.

You were born in a state of presence, without an ego. However, your ego quickly developed, and in a couple of years you obtained an identity. You learned that you have a name, gender, and a family. You began to understand that certain actions produced certain results. You realized that you had likes and dislikes, and you learned which behaviors were appropriate and inappropriate. You also began to desire material things and place a value on them. All of this learning fed your young ego.

While your ego was developing, the state of presence that you experienced at birth began to diminish. With each small advance of the maturing ego, the Present receded into the background. When the ego became fully realized, you no longer had a need to live in the Present. The higher state of awareness that you experienced at birth was transformed into a lower state of consciousness, more specifically, a form of "waking" sleep.

The Present did not leave you. *You left it.*

You were born in a state of divine presence only to lose it to the developing ego. Thus, your work lies in returning home, to the Present. There is a saying, "The truth will set you free." The Truth exists in the Present. And the Present will set you free by exposing your ego for what it really is...nothing. Your ego will die with the death of your body. The only part of you that will not die is your soul.

The Present waits for you to engage it, to

show you the Truth, to set your soul free from the shackles of the ego.

The Present awaits you.

THE KEY TO HAPPINESS

Learn to let go. That is the key to happiness.

— The Buddha

The Buddha taught that suffering occurs because you are attached to your desires. Thus, if you want to end your suffering, you must rid yourself of your attachment to the things you desire and crave.

Your desires exist only in your mind and are fueled by the ego and society. You are not born with desires; you acquire them. You are born with needs (mostly instinctive ones) such as food, water, nurturing, and shelter. If you want to end your attachment to your desires and cravings, it is important to differentiate your desires from your needs.

You need water, but the ego will desire

sparkling, bottled water. You need clothing, but the vain ego wants designer apparel. You need reliable transportation; however, the ego will crave a Mercedes or Lexus. You need adequate shelter, but oversized homes with media rooms, swimming pools, and hot tubs are the desires of the ego. Furthermore, the advertising world professes that if you purchase all you desire, your life will have more significance, more meaning, and you will be happier. Yet, the reality is quite different.

If you have the financial means to acquire the objects your ego desires, in time you find these items lose their value, leaving you wanting more. If you don't have the means to acquire them, you become disappointed, and your longing for things you can't have makes you bitter.

To be happy, you must rid yourself of desire. *You must lose your attachment to material objects.* But, how? You practice living in the Here and Now. When you are living in the Present your desires cease to exist because *you experience detachment.* Don't take my word for it. Try it, and see for yourself.

Be present and ask what it is you desire. You

won't desire anything, except maybe to live more of your life in the Present. In the Now, you discover *you already possess everything you need.* If you are in possession of everything you need, and you have no desires, are you suffering? No. *The end of suffering and the secret to happiness lie in the Present.*

THE BIG FLOOD

Faith is a knowledge within the heart, beyond the reach of proof.

— Khalil Gibran

Robert was a very religious man, a man of tremendous faith. One day there was a terrible flood, and the water around Robert's house began to rise rapidly.

While Robert stood on his porch watching the water surround his house, a gentleman in a canoe paddled by and said to Robert, "I have room in my canoe, why don't you hop in and I'll get you out of here." Robert replied, "No thank you. I am a man of great faith. God will save me."

Robert went back into his house. The water

continued to rise, flooding the first floor. Robert was forced to retreat to the second floor of his house.

As Robert looked out his bedroom window at the rising water, another gentleman in a boat paddled by. "I've got room in my boat, why don't you get in and I'll get you out of here."

Robert replied, "No thank you. I'm a man of great faith. God will save me."

The floodwaters continued to rise forcing Robert to climb onto the roof of his house. A rescue helicopter spotted Robert and called down to him, "I'm going to throw you a ladder so that you can climb into the helicopter. I'll safely get you out of here."

Once more, Robert replied, "No thanks. I'm a man of great faith. God will save me."

The floodwaters rose above Robert's house and he drowned. When Robert arrived in Heaven, he greeted God and asked, "Why didn't you save me from that horrific flood? Did I not show my tremendous faith in you?"

God replied, "What more would you have me do? I sent you two boats and a helicopter!"

The Infinite Spirit *Is*. It can be found anywhere, anytime. You become conscious of the Infinite Spirit through your soul. But, because man lives most of his days in a form of waking sleep, it can be difficult to be aware of anything other than the endless, mind-numbing, rambling thoughts of the ego.

To become aware of the Infinite Spirit, you must still your mind of all thought and become internally silent—you must become present. *When you are present, you will see that miracles are literally happening all around you, all the time.*

If Robert had been living in the Present, he would have seen God was attempting to save him. However, Robert's ego was convinced that because Robert was a man of great faith, he must be worthy of a great miracle. Robert failed to understand that the Infinite Spirit is always available, always offering assistance. If you raise your level of conscious awareness, you will see *the Infinite Spirit is always at your immediate disposal, always ready and willing to help you, too.*

If you are currently in the midst of "a great flood" in your own life, ask the Infinite Spirit for assistance. Then, be present and patient. You will receive an answer. Don't let your ego judge the answer, as was the case with Robert. Robert's vanity convinced him he was destined for something far greater than a boat, canoe, or helicopter. In the end, Robert's vanity was his downfall, ultimately leading him to his death.

Have faith and trust in the Infinite Spirit, for it knows all and is always ready and willing to offer you assistance. On the other hand, allowing your ego to dictate your decisions often results in more problems, and quite possibly, death.

MASTER YOUR FATE

I am the master of my fate:
I am the captain of my soul.

— William Henley

If you desire to be the master of your fate and the captain of your soul, you must live in the Present; otherwise your ego will be the master of your fate. The ego exists in a world of duality and subjectivity, where it demands to be the center of attention. Moreover, the ego is fearful and sees threats to its existence everywhere. *If you are making choices based in fear, then fear is controlling you.* You cannot be the master of something you cannot control.

You have the power to overcome your fears, worries, and negative thoughts by making the effort to live in the Present. *In the Present you realize the only limits you have are the ones self-imposed.*

The ego separates you from the Divine. The moment you begin to think, you leave the Now and enter the world of the ego and false personality where you no longer view yourself as a spiritual Being, but as a physical being. When this occurs, you begin to partake of the imaginary suffering that exists in the physical world. If you are not in the Now, you are living a life of limited consciousness and awareness, separated from the Infinite Spirit.

When you are living in the Present, you experience union with the Divine and gain access to higher wisdom and understanding. *The Present reveals all is possible with God.* When you live in conscious harmony with the Infinite Spirit you become the master of your fate and the captain of your soul.

REALIZE YOUR FULL POTENTIAL

What lies behind us and what lies before us are tiny matters compared to what lies within us.

— Ralph Waldo Emerson

When you live in the Present, you access another dimension of time and space and experience a higher state of consciousness. In the Present you possess an intense awareness, divine intuition, and universal understanding. The Present is an infinite, boundless place consisting of unconditional love and acceptance, where miracles are commonplace and duality, judgment, and suffering cease to exist.

In the Present you escape the confines of the cellular world (the world of the body, ego, and form) and enter the molecular world (the world of the soul) where you gain the knowledge and understanding that everything, including you, consists solely of energy vibrating at different frequencies, and everything is always in a constant state of motion. Furthermore, you awaken to the divine realization that you are not merely human, but more importantly, you are a spiritual Being—a soul born of God, the Infinite Spirit, the Creator of all that exists. In the Present you experience the same rebirth and awakening Jesus experienced.

Jesus knew he was the biological son of Mary, but he also knew his soul was born from something more spiritually evolved than his mother. Jesus awoke to the realization that his soul was born of the Universal Soul—God. It was the strength of His spiritual knowledge, understanding, and being that allowed Jesus to perform miracles. Furthermore, Jesus states you and I are capable of performing miracles, too.

Afterward the disciples asked Jesus privately, "Why couldn't we cast out that demon?" "You don't have enough faith," Jesus told them. "I

> *tell you the truth, if you had faith even as small*
> *as a mustard seed, you could say to this*
> *mountain, 'Move from here to there,' and it*
> *would move. Nothing would be impossible."*

Matthew 17:19-20

Jesus makes it very clear to His disciples that their inability to perform miracles is the direct result of their lack of faith in knowing whom they really are and what they are truly capable of doing. Moreover, the slightest bit of doubt prevents the miraculous from occurring in your own life, and hinders your ability to access your unlimited potential. Doubt prevents you from chasing your dreams. Doubt binds you to the cellular world and the ego, and prevents you from experiencing the glory of the Present. Doubt is responsible for more failures than successes.

What if there was a world in which doubt and failure did not exist? What if you lived in a world where miracles were commonplace? What if, whatever you attempted, you succeeded? Would you settle for anything less than greatness? No, you probably would not. Yet, this is exactly what so many do. The very slightest doubt or fear of not being able to accomplish something extraordinary obliterates any effort and destroys our will and desire. The world that I mention does exist. It is not fantasy. This world is the Present, the eternal Now.

When you live in the Present, you live in conscious harmony with the Universe and God. In the physical world, fear and doubt have tremendous power. In the Present, fear and doubt do not exist; they are merely words.

If you are not living in the Present, your ego and false personality dictate your thoughts and actions. You identify with your body, and believe your thoughts are real. You become concerned with your appearance and what others think. You lose touch with your spiritual nature and allow outside forces to dictate your choices. Fear, doubt, and the limitations they automatically impose dominate your thinking. Hence, your potential never becomes fully realized.

Imagine you have in your hand a 150 watt, three-way, light bulb. If you hold the light bulb in your hand, it is just a light bulb. It is not emitting any light. It has the capability to accomplish more, to be more, but if it remains in your hand, it will never be more than metal filaments encased in glass, and really is of no benefit whatsoever.

Suppose you installed the 150 watt, three-way bulb into a three-way lamp. Without any power to the lamp, the light bulb is still filaments and glass. Without electricity, the light bulb is useless.

Now, suppose you add power to the lamp and turn its switch once. The bulb emits 50 watts of light. At this setting, the bulb is functioning as it was intended. However, since it is capable of emitting 150 watts, it is only living up to a third its potential. Turn the switch once more, and the light bulb emits 100 watts. It is living up to two-thirds its full potential. Turn the switch one last time, and the bulb emits 150 watts. The light bulb is now functioning at its maximum potential.

The light bulb's creator gave it the capability to emit up to 150 watts, and given the right circumstances (a three-way lamp and electricity), the bulb shines in all its 150 watt glory. In this analogy the lamp represents your body, the three-way switch represents your ego, and the light bulb is your soul.

If you do not take care of yourself physically, mentally, and emotionally, you will become the equivalent of a poor functioning lamp—prone to breaking often (illness), in need of replacement parts (surgery), and constant servicing (doctor visits and medication).

Continuing with this example, let us assume that all lamps (bodies) are created with light bulbs in them (souls). What prevents the bulb (soul) from emitting light (awakening)? The lamp's switch (the ego) performs this function.

When you were born, you consisted of a body and soul. At birth, your soul was present, peering through your eyes in a state of wonder and fascination. As you grew, your ego developed and you learned you had a name, parents, gender, likes and dislikes, and physical and emotional needs. You were taught certain behaviors were right or wrong. With your ego and personality continuing to develop and becoming stronger and more pronounced, your soul slowly receded into the background, until it was eventually lulled to sleep. This typically occurs around preadolescence. Continuing with my analogy, you were born emitting 150 watts of light, meaning your soul was present; it was wide-awake. Over time, your ego grew and your soul receded into the background, dimming the light emitted from the bulb. Between nine and twelve years of age, the light was turned off, meaning your soul had fallen asleep.

Your spiritual work is to peel away the false personality of the ego so that your soul can rightfully shine again. You do this by ridding yourself of negative thoughts—worry, anxiety, fear, guilt, doubt, imagination—and making the effort to live in the Present.

To provide an environment for your soul to emerge and do divine work, you must take care of your body and your mind, for it is the only instrument the soul has in which to perform its work. As you become healthy in body and mind, you create a solid foundation upon which you can begin your spiritual work—the peeling away of the false personality of the ego. As your ego slowly recedes and the soul awakens from its slumber, you begin to fulfill your destiny as a creative, spiritual Being with unlimited potential and possibilities.

LETTING GO OF SUFFERING

People have a hard time letting go of their suffering. Out of a fear of the unknown, they prefer suffering that is familiar.

— Thich Nhat Hanh

Individuals suffer due to perceived problems occurring in time, in the world forms. In the Now, these problems disappear because a majority of suffering is not real—it is imaginary. *You only suffer when you are not present, when you are not living in the Now.* If you possessed the knowledge that living in the Present would put an end to your suffering, would you still choose to suffer?

Many people hold on to their suffering (some actually thrive on it) because suffering makes them feel alive and gives them a sense of identity.

Personally, I view this as a form of mental illness. It is insane to choose suffering if you can be at peace. Yet, I know many people who refuse to give up their suffering because it defines them. Within minutes of meeting them, they tell you of their problems: relationship problems, physical problems, problems at work, financial problems, and so on. Misery loves company, so we often relate to others based on mutual problems and shared experiences. Have you watched your local news lately? It is probably 90 percent negative. The recession, record unemployment, crime, housing foreclosures, the budget deficit…the list seems endless. It is nearly impossible not to identify with all the problems in the U.S. and abroad when it is almost all you hear these days. Try an experiment. For one day, don't read the newspaper or watch the news. And, if anyone mentions anything negative to you, gently change the subject to something positive. I bet you will find your stress and anxiety is less that day. Of course *the absolute, best stress reliever is to be present.*

If you are not living in the Now, you are allowing the ego to be the dominant, driving force in your life and the ego thrives on problems and suffering because they validate the ego's existence. If your ego is in charge, you will have problems and experience suffering — I guarantee it. *When you are living in time and tied to the world of forms, you are the ego and all its perceptions, thoughts, problems, and accompanying suffering.*

The ego is your soul's nemesis. It will attempt anything and everything to keep you identified with your problems and living in fear, because this prevents you from being in the Now. Conversely, the Now is your ego's nemesis. The Now reveals the truth regarding the ego and its problems and suffering — *they are nothing but an illusion.*

When you are present you possess unconditional acceptance of your life circumstances. Nothing is bad or good, everything is just as it should be. When you are living in the Present you release your suffering and experience inner peace.

THE SECOND COMING

The kingdom of God is within you.

— The Bible

Jesus was a man who died on the cross. Christ is the awakened, enlightened soul of Jesus that lives in the eternal Now. Being an immortal soul, Christ will not return because He never left. *We left Him.*

Christ exists in the Now, outside of time. Because we are confined to time and space by the ego, we think He will return. The ego cannot comprehend living outside its own self, or outside of time in the eternal Now.

Christ is not returning to save you. *You must save yourself by coming to Him* through living in the Present, by existing in the same infinite space that Christ and God exist. *Thus, the second coming of Christ is the awakening of your soul.*

During the Last Supper, Jesus asks if His disciples cannot at least stay awake with Him for one hour. Consider the following…the disciples were not literally falling asleep. The problem was *they could not remain present with Jesus in the eternal Now.* Let me explain.

Suppose someone dear to you is terminally ill and has been told they have 24 hours to live. They tell you they don't want to fall asleep with so little time remaining, and ask if you would remain awake with them for their remaining hours on Earth. Do you think you would selfishly fall asleep under these incredible circumstances? I doubt it. But, apparently Jesus's disciples were literally dozing off at the Last Supper, on the eve of their Teacher's impending death. I doubt that, too. The Bible is full of metaphors and symbolism, and there is a message behind the story of the disciples' inability to remain awake at the Last Supper.

Jesus is telling his disciples to resist the temptation to express negativity, fear, and imagination regarding His impending death, and to *try to remain present with*

Him. Jesus was spiritually awake, living in the Now, and was asking His disciples to be awake and in the Now with Him in His final hours. However, some of the disciples were struggling to remain present with Jesus. The other message in this story is it takes a great effort to be present, to remain in the Now for an extended amount of time.

In the Bible Jesus says, "Seek and you will find." Don't waste precious time waiting for Jesus to return to save you. *Be present and seek Him right now.*

THE LAW OF RECURRENCE

The Law of Recurrence is a universal law that states that circumstances and events occur repeatedly (recur) until a conscious effort is made to break the pattern. These patterns occur, not only in one's life, but also over lifetimes and generations.

The Law of Recurrence can be seen in the universe, nature, and man. The Moon orbiting the Earth every 28 days, the Earth orbiting the Sun every 365 days, and Haley's comet being visible every 75 or 76 years are a few examples. In nature it can be seen in the migratory patterns of the monarch butterfly and the humpback whale, and the spawning of ocean coral. Recurring patterns can be found everywhere, however, I specifically want to focus on the Law of Recurrence as it pertains to you.

Because man lives most of his life in a state of waking sleep, his unconscious actions create patterns that typically are not broken until he begins to make an effort to live in the Present. These unconscious patterns, or recurrences, often have an adverse effect.

Have you known someone who seems to go from one bad relationship to the next? Or, someone who skips from job to job, and never stays with one long enough to move ahead? Do you know someone who is always about to become ultra-rich selling the latest, multi-level marketing product? Do you know someone who is always giving to others, but totally neglects their own needs? Have you observed patterns of physical, sexual, or substance abuse passing from generation to generation in families? All of these situations are due to the Law of Recurrence.

You can break free from the Law of Recurrence, however, first you must become aware of how it manifests in your own life. This requires that you begin observing yourself. If you can bring presence into your life, you can start to objectively observe the unconscious decisions you make that create and maintain harmful, recurring patterns of behavior.

A couple of years ago I had a female client who was distraught because her relationships with men never lasted more than a few months, and always ended with her getting hurt. She was attractive, smart, and had a great job. I could not see any immediate reason why she could not have a lasting relationship. I asked her to objectively look at her life and possibly determine why she was stuck in this repeating pattern of failed relationships.

Over the course of several sessions it became apparent that she was projecting onto her relationships the foregone conclusion that it would end badly for her. She assumed she would get hurt before the relationship had a chance to succeed. Her critical self was sabotaging her relationships. My client's fear of getting hurt became a self-fulfilling prophecy. *You attract the very thing you fear the most.*

My client later realized her fear was rooted in the fact that her father divorced her mother when my client was a young child. Her father shortly remarried, and had several children with his new wife. Her father became more involved with his new family, and neglected his duties as the father to my client. In addition, my client's mother never remarried and remained very bitter towards her ex-husband.

In her adult relationships with men, my client was perpetuating the Law of Recurrence by recreating her father abandoning her as a child. She would expect her boyfriend to leave her just as her primary, male role model left her when she was a child and needed him most.

We spent several sessions being present to her childhood memories. In time, she realized that her father's leaving had nothing to do with her. However, her ego had suffered a great loss in its early childhood development, convincing her she was not worthy of a man's love.

Our work in the Present allowed my client to break free of her ego's belief that she was not worthy of a great, loving relationship with a man. We worked on consciously projecting into the universe that she was worthy of finding a loving person who would remain in her life, that a successful, wonderful relationship was in her near future, and that she was ready to receive it when it manifested. (About a year after our last session, my client called to say that she had found the most wonderful man and they were getting engaged.)

Everyone can find examples of the Law of Recurrence in their lives. Some of the patterns we unconsciously create are benign, however some of them prevent us from creating the life we desire and deserve. If you are experiencing difficulties in certain areas of your life, look to see if it is due to the Law of Recurrence.

BEING PRESENT WITH CHILDREN

Children will not remember you for the material things you provided but for the feeling that you cherished them.

— Richard L. Evans

When you are present you experience life from the highest part of yourself—your soul. The soul, by its very nature, cannot express negativity; it is impossible. The soul is unconditional love and acceptance. This is what you offer anyone with whom you are present. This is why it is important to be present with your children.

How frequently do you speak to your children while you are engaged in another activity? Children can tell if you aren't really listening to them. Try to make the effort each time you speak to your children to stop whatever you are doing in that moment, be present, and focus solely on them.

When you are present with your child, you eliminate any interference or thinking from the ego, and you really listen. In giving your full attention and listening objectively, they will feel love and respect because they will sense they are important and that you are not judging them. Moreover, children often say one thing when they mean something else. By listening to them in a state of presence, you have a greater chance of catching the "message behind the message" if it exists.

When your child realizes they can tell you anything without feeling judged, you allow them *to be*. Show them love and respect, and acknowledge that what they have to say is important to you. Be present with your child as much as possible. It will pay huge dividends in your relationship with them, their personal growth, and their self-esteem.

TRANSFORMING REAL SUFFERING

The way in which a man accepts his fate and all the suffering it entails, the way in which he takes up his cross, gives him ample opportunity—even under the most difficult circumstances—to add a deeper meaning to his life.

— Viktor Frankl

Nothing happens to any man that he is not formed by nature to bear.

— Marcus Aurelius

Most of the suffering you experience is not real, *it exists in your imagination.* You have been conditioned, through fear, to suffer over events or circumstances that have not occurred. The mere possibility of something bad occurring in your life is enough to create copious amounts of anxiety and worry, and consequently, a tremendous loss of valuable time and energy—energy that ultimately could be used to assist you in living in the Now.

While most of your suffering is imaginary, you will experience moments of real suffering. *You have the ability to transform real suffering into spiritual growth.* Imaginary suffering is unnecessary and feeds your ego, while the transformation of real suffering furthers your growth and evolution as a spiritual Being.

Real suffering occurs with events of great magnitude, for example, the death of a family member or dear friend, the demise of a long marriage, or losing all of your belongings in a natural disaster. Basically, real suffering is associated with events that do not happen frequently. A simple test to determine whether or not your suffering is real is to ask, "Would this suffering disappear if I were to discover I just won $120 million dollars in the lottery?" If the answer is yes, then your suffering is not real. Another test involves being present. If your suffering disappears when you are living in the Now, your suffering is not real.

How do you transform real suffering?

You surrender to it. By surrendering, you allow your suffering to penetrate every cell of your body. When you are able to totally surrender to your suffering with every ounce of your Being, at that precise moment, *you will find God.* And when you do, you will realize that physically you are nothing, but spiritually you are everything. You will know and understand the meaning and reason for your existence. And, when that moment occurs, write it down, commit it to memory, and never let a day go by where you don't remind yourself of it. And, you will discover that the transformation of real suffering has given you the most wonderful gift of all.

Real suffering provides you the opportunity to increase the consciousness of your soul. And, if you are grieving over the loss of a loved one, what better a way to remember them, than to transform the pain of their passing into spiritual growth.

BE HERE NOW

You must live in the present, launch yourself on every wave, find your eternity in each moment.

— Henry David Thoreau

Every moment of presence you experience consists of both a death and re-birth. In the conscious awareness of the Now, that which is false in you dies, and your soul awakens as you are re-born into your true nature — *your Being, your oneness with the Infinite Spirit that created all and permeates all that exists.*

People often tell me that under different circumstances they could make more of an effort to be present. What most fail to realize is that you already have in your possession everything you need to live in the Now. You do not need to set aside time each day to be present or to meditate. It is not necessary to fast, visit Nepal, sell all your belongings, or join a monastery. Sure, you might find some temporary benefit from making drastic lifestyle changes, but in all likelihood the effects from these changes will be short-lived.

The key point is *you must make the effort to be present regardless of your circumstances or environment.* By divine creation, you have already been given all you need to awaken. All you must do is bring total awareness and attention to whatever you are doing right now. It is not easy, but you can do it. And if you want to spiritually grow and awaken your soul, then *you must do it.*

Be here now.

Leave behind all that is false, for the light and love that you will awaken into and radiate as a spiritual Being. In the glorious Present, you will see that love is all there is—that the Infinite Spirit is simply...*Love.* And then you will understand another simple, yet divine Truth—*it is in Love that you awaken, and it is through Love that you become enlightened.*

CREATIVITY & DIVINE INSPIRATION

As soon as you trust yourself, you will know how to live.

— Goethe

Have you ever noticed that many of your most creative ideas occurred when you were living in the Present? Real creativity occurs when one is in conscious harmony with their higher self. In these moments, there is a direct connection between you and the Infinite Spirit. Can you be creative and not be in the Now? Of course, you can. However, creativity born from the ego versus creativity born from your higher self, differs greatly.

Creativity that arises from divine inspiration is of a much higher caliber and quality than creativity born of the ego. Creativity arising from the ego typically lacks originality, as it often is based upon or builds upon the ideas of someone else. Consequently, this level of creativity is generally characterized as mediocre. On the other hand, real creativity is original, sincere, and truthful, and retains these qualities over time. Leonardo da Vinci's *Mona Lisa*, Walt Whitman's *Song of Myself*, and Johann Sebastian Bach's *Brandenburg Concertos* are several examples.

In addition to moments when you are present, there are two periods in the day when you are especially susceptible to receiving divine inspiration: just before you fall asleep and just before you wake up. If there is a situation occurring in your life where you feel you need guidance or inspiration from the Infinite Spirit, try the following exercise.

Just before you go to bed, ask the Infinite Spirit for assistance regarding a specific situation. Then, let it go. As your body relaxes and prepares to enter into sleep, your breathing and heart rate will slow down and your mind will become quiet. There is a window of time just before you fall asleep, in which you will feel disassociated from your body. It is often in this small window of time you will suddenly receive the answer. I believe it is divine inspiration. This same window of opportunity occurs in the morning just before you fully awaken from sleeping. So many times have I received divine inspiration in these moments that I placed a notepad and pen next to my bed to record them.

Real creativity occurs when you are present. In those moments, you rise above your ego and consciously connect to your soul. You then become an open vessel for receiving divine inspiration and guidance from Above.

USE THE PRESENT TO HEAL THE PAST

Those who are free of resentful thoughts surely find peace.

> — The Buddha

Nobody can bring you peace but yourself.

> — Ralph Waldo Emerson

Being present has numerous psychological, emotional, and physical benefits. I have directly observed how living in the Now actually slows down the aging process. And, modern psychology is finally recognizing the benefits to living in the Now.

"Mindfulness" is the term many psychologists and psychotherapists use to denote an awareness and acceptance of the present moment. The opposite of mindfulness is preoccupation. Today there are many books on mindfulness and its practical application in treating anxiety, depression, obsessive-compulsive disorders, phobias, chronic pain, post-traumatic stress disorder, and insomnia. I specifically want to discuss *how to use the power of the Present to heal painful events in your past.*

First, being in the Now offers you an objective perspective regarding the past, and presents you with an opportunity to accept and forgive painful situations and the individuals involved. Second, in healing the past you heal your future self.

If you have experienced a painful event in your past and you are holding on to it, it is time to let it go. Holding on to the past prevents you from healing emotionally and advancing spiritually. In order to move forward *you must heal the past.*

Suppose you had a fight many years ago with someone dear to you and it has affected your relationship ever since. First, take a moment and be present. While maintaining presence, revisit the negative encounter. Become very aware of everything concerning this past event. Pay close attention to the behaviors, actions, and feelings that occurred with you, your friend or family member, and anyone else who may have been involved. By being in the Now and intentionally revisiting the past, you are able to view the situation with detachment, and hopefully gain a new perspective and understanding regarding what actually occurred. This process can be very powerful. You may realize it wasn't the event that has caused the pain and suffering, *but your reaction to it.* Remember, nothing can hurt you unless you allow it. When you are able to intentionally view a past event with presence, you gain the ability to accept and forgive those involved. You may even realize that moving forward requires forgiving yourself.

To heal the past through presence is empowering and gives you the opportunity to release painful events that may be preventing you from moving forward emotionally and spiritually. It is also possible to heal the past with individuals who are deceased. However, because you have chosen to heal a past event, it does not mean the other individuals involved will do the same. The ego is often unwilling to let go of its suffering and reluctant to forgive anyone of wrongdoings it has endured. Yet, you do not have to allow the choices of others to keep you stuck in the past.

Lastly, I want to talk about healing your future self. Remember, when you live with your ego dictating your thoughts and actions, you live tied to linear time. As such, you view the events in your life as occurring in a straight line; certain events occurred at specific ages in your life or during specific years. The soul, however, exists outside of man-made, linear time. When your soul is present to a past moment in your life, and you heal that moment, from that point on *you are no longer the same person. The past moment that you healed affects every moment occurring after it, even those moments that are still in the past.* So, by healing the past you begin to heal your future self.

A SPIRITUAL PERSPECTIVE ON DEATH

My religion is to live and die without regret.

—Milarepa

It is not death that a man should fear, but he should fear never beginning to live.

—Marcus Aurelius

If you live each day a slave to the ego, death is a terrible, traumatic event that you will face with trepidation and fear, totally oblivious to the possibilities it presents. On the other hand, those individuals who pursue a spiritual path often come to the realization death is nothing to fear, death is the final test in a lifetime of efforts to live free from the desires and impulses of the ego and the body. From a spiritual and philosophical standpoint, death is a teacher, the greatest teacher, for it teaches us that our time in this body is finite, precious, and not to be wasted.

If you begin each day with the understanding that today could be the last day of your life, you will be more inclined to spend the day wisely. This perspective does not give you license to shun responsibility. To spend time wisely is to live each moment of the day in conscious harmony, engaging your soul in the eternal Present. In other words, *live each moment with purpose and with intentional awareness.* This means whatever you find yourself doing in the current moment, *really do it.* If you want to shout, shout at the top of your lungs. If you want to cry, cry until every tear is shed. If you want to tell someone how much you love them, look into their eyes and tell them with all the love in your heart. If you want to take a walk, really experience walking. Take your shoes off. Feel the earth under your feet. If you are feeling joyful, let the joy radiate from the depth of your soul to every cell of your body.

You have in your possession the one thing you need to make each minute, each hour, and each day the most wonderful, most glorious of your entire life—*your soul*. And the more you engage your soul the more you will understand that no matter where you are and no matter what you are doing, that just being here, right now, in this moment, is what matters most of all. And, as you spend more time in the eternal Now, *you will realize that each moment of presence makes your life fuller and richer than you could possibly have imagined.*

HEAVEN AND HELL

Hell and heaven are states of mind, not places.

— Meher Baba

Heaven and hell are an illusion; they are subjective states of consciousness. Once you realize you are an immortal soul, you will gain the understanding that death, too, is an illusion. From the soul's perspective, death, heaven, and hell do not exist. *You create your own heaven and hell.*

Be present right now.

Do you see that in the Present duality does not exist? Without duality, there is no right or wrong, good or bad, and no heaven or hell. Everything just *is.* Do you now see heaven and hell are subjective states of consciousness tied to the physical world?

If you are not living in the eternal Now, your

existence alternates between relative states of heaven or hell depending on your state of mind. If you are feeling negative and believe your suffering, worry, and fear are real, and you act and react accordingly, then you are in your own personal hell. Conversely, if you are having a wonderful day, and you are feeling happy to be alive, and loving everything in your life, then in that moment you are in your own personal heaven.

In the Now, happiness and misery cease to exist, and you realize that heaven and hell are subjective states based solely on your mental, emotional, and physical well-being at that precise moment in your life. *The only thing real in this world is your soul as it exists in the Eternal Present.* Everything else is an illusion.

YOUR BEING ATTRACTS YOUR LIFE

Every problem has a gift for you in its hands

— R chard Bach

Your *Being* is the sum total of all that you (body, soul, and spirit) are and have experienced up to this very moment in your life. Moreover, your Being is composed of numerous sub-levels of being. At these sub-levels, *being is your ability to live what you understand.*

Those with *little being* in a certain area generally are restricted to solely possessing *knowledge* about a given subject or activity. Your level of being increases as you move from knowing something to understanding it. Finally, when you are able to put into practice and live what you understand, you are said to have *being* in that area.

Your Being attracts your life.

This means everything occurring in your life is happening for a reason. Your level of being regarding relationships, money, health, and so on, attracts into your life the lessons or knowledge you specifically need in order to grow. If you are experiencing difficulty with certain areas of your life or with certain people, it is because *you attracted it*. Thus, it is important to ask, "Why is this happening to me? What am I to learn from this?"

Steve and Lynn's marriage was falling apart. Lynn felt alone in the marriage because Steve was always working, and made little time to be with her. Steve was very successful in business and provided Lynn with everything she could possibly need: a beautiful home, a nice car, clothes, a housekeeper, and so on.

Steve had been married twice before, and his previous wives had divorced him for the same reason—he didn't invest enough in the marriage to make it work. Lynn did not want to divorce Steve, but was going to if things did not change, and soon.

Steve's level of being in business matters was exceptional. Consequently, he attracted into his life a great deal of success and money. However, when it came to being successful as a husband, Steve's level of being was lacking. As a result, he was on his third marriage. Steve realized he needed help or divorce was imminent.

Over the course of several months and with the aid of a counselor, Steve began to realize what was required to maintain a healthy, loving, lasting marriage and he put into practice his new understanding. His level of being as a husband grew, and now Steve and Lynn have a wonderful marriage.

If you are encountering problems in certain areas of your life, it is for a reason. Ask yourself, "Why is this happening to me? What do I need to learn from this?" As was the case with Steve, you may find you need to address your level of being. If so, take the necessary steps to acquire the knowledge and understanding you need to move forward in your life.

UNLEASH YOUR SOUL

*Whatever you do, or dream you can, begin it.
Boldness has genius and power and magic in
it.*

— Goethe

Hitch your wagon to a star.

—Ralph Waldo Emerson

If you believe you are the mind and body you will remain confined to the material world. You, however, have a soul and it is through the soul that you experience the Infinite Spirit. It is through the mind and body that you experience and interact in the world of forms, and it is through the soul that you experience and interact in the spiritual world.

There is a quote from *The Emerald Tablet of*

Hermes, "That which is Below corresponds to that which is Above, and that which is Above, corresponds to that which is Below, to accomplish the miracles of the One Thing."

Many people are familiar with the abbreviated version, "As above, so below." The meaning of the quote is simple—the microcosm (man and the earth) is a direct reflection of the macrocosm (God and the heavens). I would like to modify the quote a bit further and state, *"As it is on the inside, so it is on the outside."* In other words, your inner state (thoughts and consciousness) determines your outer state (reality). Your thoughts and level of consciousness directly affect your body, emotions, and behavior; they determine your reality.

Whether you are having negative thoughts and expressing negative emotions, or feeling happy and expressing joy, your body, behavior, and the individuals around you will respond accordingly. Negativity attracts negativity, joy attracts joy, and your awakened soul attracts the Divine. Your soul is a morsel of the Infinite Spirit. As such, your soul has the characteristics, powers, and abilities of its Creator.

If you allow negative thinking to control or decide your course of action, you allow the ego to enslave the soul. However, you have the ability to rise above the limited thinking of the mind and ego. When you are present, the soul speaks and acts through you. The work of the soul is the greatest endeavor you can embark upon in your lifetime. When you are in the Now and living in conscious harmony, you free the soul from the ego's restraints and experience the miraculous Present.

ENVELOPING OTHERS WITH DIVINE LOVE

Love one another and help others to rise to the higher levels, simply by pouring out love. Love is infectious and the greatest healing energy.

— Sai Baba

As a God-realized soul living in the eternal Present, you have the ability to work wonders. All it requires is intention, affirmation, and faith.

It is through the soul that you experience and communicate with God. In a state of presence, your thoughts and words are very powerful because you are purposely bringing a higher level of consciousness, or divine awareness, to them via your soul and its connection to God. You can liken it to a higher or deeper level of prayer. The following exercise is just one of many in which you can utilize the power of the soul. I call it *enveloping others with divine Love.*

Think of a person or object you would like to envelop with divine Love. It can be anyone or anything, someone alive or deceased, someone living far away—anything that you can imagine that you would like to surround with conscious Love. *Be very specific in your choice.* Next, become very present and conscious of the Now.

With your object clearly in focus, imagine a giant orb filled with the Light and Love of God. Imagine the orb intentionally and with great precision, enveloping the person or object you have chosen, saturating them in God's Love. While you are doing this, note how wonderful it is for your chosen object to receive God's Love. Keep the orb of God's Love enveloping its recipient for as long as you like. If you choose someone who is ill or who is in need of some form of healing, imagine the loving energy helping and curing the person of his or her affliction.

The next two steps are very important.

Now, *you must affirm the process.* It is imperative you state aloud, in past tense, what has just occurred.

You are declaring that something is factual, that *it has happened.* Also, it is important that you not claim ownership of the gift. It is not your love, it is God's Love working through you. For example, "My son received the loving, healing energy of the Infinite Spirit," or "The Earth was bathed in divine Love." It is important that you state this aloud as though it is a known fact.

Last, *you must believe in the process. You must have faith in the power of divine Love.* You don't need to tell anyone what you are doing—be an invisible force of Love. Believe that your soul is a vessel for the Infinite Spirit to embrace others with the healing, loving energy of our divine Creator.

THE EYE OF THE STORM

To the mind that is still, the whole universe surrenders.

—Lao Tzu

Having lived near the Texas Gulf Coast, I have experienced several hurricanes. One unique feature to these incredible forces of Nature is that strong hurricanes have a well-developed eye at their center. The defining characteristic of the eye of a hurricane is that it is an area of calm activity—little to no rain, minimal wind, and sunny, often cloudless, skies. The outer bands of a hurricane are capable of creating massive destruction, but the eye of the storm is calm. In life, to be the "eye of the storm" is *to be present amidst the chaos surrounding you.*

If you are experiencing a difficult time in your

life, do not forget you have a choice regarding how to respond. If you choose to allow your ego to identify with all the chaos, express negativity, and blame others for your problems, then do so. Own that decision. But, I assure you, your problems will not go away. They will recur until you are ready to be present to your life, until you possess the desire to gain an objective understanding of how and why your problems keep occurring. It is through living in the Now that you become the master of your life. Without presence, you remain a slave to the thoughts, negativity, and emotional whims of the ego.

So, if your life is filled with turmoil, you have a choice—you can remain in the outer bands of the hurricane and be a slave to the destructive power of the ego, or you can be the calming, still presence of the eye of the storm, and make the efforts necessary to become the master of your life.

LIVING AUTHENTICALLY

He who knows others is wise; he who knows himself is enlightened.

— Lao Tzu

To thine own self be true.

— Shakespeare

Many individuals seek my services because they are unhappy. It is common for my clients to come to the realization that their life lacks *authenticity*. In other words, they aren't living their life in accordance with their values and beliefs. They do things they don't want or shouldn't, and they don't do the things they want or should.

What does it mean to be authentic?

To be authentic is *to be true to yourself.* However, to be true to yourself requires that you know who you are—not who you think you are, or who you think you want to be—but who you really are, at your core. *To know yourself is to know who you are when all the layers of false personality have been stripped away.*

How do you be true to yourself when all about you is false? By living in the Present.

The Present reveals the objective truth. Once you are present ask the following, "What brings me joy? What do I value? What is truly important to me? What changes do I need to make in my life to live the life I truly desire?"

Your subjective ego, consumed with its own identity, will address these questions from its own vain perspective, and its answers will typically concern material items that provide comfort, power, and prestige. But, your objective soul will be honest, truthful, and sincere. Your soul's answers to these questions may surprise you. *Pay close attention to these answers.*

Once you realize the truth regarding who you really are and what truly matters to you, you must take the necessary steps to incorporate these truths into your daily existence. In time, you will find you are living authentically and harmoniously.

FEAR

Fear brings about that which one is afraid of.
—Viktor Frankl

Fear is the source of all negativity. It is the root of all conflict and anxiety, and the source of all jealousy, bigotry, envy, and hatred. Where living in the Now benefits the soul, fear benefits and fuels the ego. Fear stifles your creativity, and causes you to make choices that you don't want to. Fear can debilitate and imprison you. Most importantly, fear prevents you from being an immortal, creative, spiritual Being entitled to a life of infinite peace and joy.

All fear is learned. At a young age you are taught what and what not to fear. Not only do you inherit your parent's fears, you take on the fears of your peers and society, the fears of your religion, even the fears of your country. When you make de-cisions based in fear, you often resent them, and in time, may come to regret those choices. It is not natural to live in fear.

If you want to understand the nature of fear, *be present*. You will observe that fear does not exist in the Now, *because fear is an illusion, it is not real.*

If you are fearful, you are allowing your ego to dictate your actions. When you act out of fear, you are not in conscious harmony with the Infinite Spirit. Fear prevents you from being in touch with your higher, spiritual self — your soul.

Your soul is God, and God is Love. You, as a God-realized soul, were created by the Infinite Spirit to be Love. So, honor your Creator and your soul by living in the Present. Don't allow fear to deprive you of what is divinely and rightfully yours. *Live from your soul and be a force of divine Love in your life and in the life of others.* A world of infinite peace, joy, and harmony awaits you.

GENERATIONAL RECURRENCE

It is easier to prevent bad habits than to break them.

— Benjamin Franklin

Earlier, I mentioned the Law of Recurrence and discussed how to detect the destructive patterns in your life created by the ego. I now want to address how this universal law can be observed in your family history, spanning generations. In order to break free of the Law of Recurrence, you must first learn what it is and realize its influence in your life.

To reiterate, the Law of Recurrence is a universal law stating that circumstances and events in your life will repeat until you make a conscious effort to observe the behavioral patterns and intentionally break them. Previously, I mentioned the Law of Recurrence in relation to the patterns you create *in this lifetime*. However, this universal law is also applicable on a much larger scale. Some of the patterns you repeat in this lifetime began prior to your birth. In other words, *you inherited them.*

Examine your genealogy and you will find examples of the Law of Recurrence. Some instances will be harmless and amusing, while others will be important and worth noting. The key point to remember is *patterns aid in keeping us asleep to our lives because they are familiar and comforting to the ego.*

Trivial examples of the Law of Recurrence over generations can be observed in the birth order of children. Important examples may include patterns of physical, emotional and sexual abuse, bankruptcy, divorce, addiction, depression, and suicide. If you are the victim of abuse, or you are aware of certain addictions occurring in your family history, you have the power to end the cycle of abuse and conquer the addiction.

Several years ago I met Raymond, a man in his

late 40's who was seeking help for anger management. Due to his uncontrollable rage, he "lost it" at work and physically assaulted a co-worker. Raymond's employer had already informed him that his anger at work was becoming problematic. This latest incident resulted in his immediate termination. Shortly afterward, his finances were in shambles and his marriage destroyed. Raymond's anger was so severe no one would hire him. He was a couple of months from running completely out of money. Raymond had already lost his house to the bank and was currently living month to month in an efficiency apartment. Raymond informed me that if things did not change quickly, he would no longer be able to pay his rent. He expected to be homeless in two or three months.

A local, non-profit agency had offered to pay for six counseling sessions for Raymond. I soon learned in our sessions that Raymond's father and grand-father had horrible tempers, too. Raymond's father had been physically abusive towards Raymond, and their relationship had been severed many years ago. Raymond did not know the whereabouts of his father, or if he was still alive.

Raymond's anger was debilitating and ultimately he allowed it to prevent me from assisting him. Despite his six sessions being paid by an outside source, Raymond terminated our therapeutic relationship after his third session. Raymond's life of anger was complicated. Six sessions of therapy would have been but a fraction of the time needed to help him. I mention Raymond because the Law of Recurrence was a key factor in understanding the reason for his destructive anger. Unfortunately, Raymond was not ready or willing to address his problem.

I encourage you to research your own genealogy for examples of the Law of Recurrence. You may find instances of this universal law that will shed light on certain behaviors or decisions you, or members of your family, have made or continue to make. More importantly, you may find patterns of generational behavior that are limiting you or preventing you from living a more fulfilling life.

RELEASE YOUR INNER BUDDHA

To be enlightened is to be one with all things.

— Dogen

The Buddha taught that everyone has the capability to become Buddhas—*to become enlightened*. To become a Buddha is to realize the divine Truth—*we are all connected, we are all one*. When you arrive at this realization, compassion for everyone and everything naturally occurs, including compassion for yourself.

There are many spiritual practices and paths upon which you can embark and become enlightened, including the practice of living in the Present. When you live in the Present, your ego disappears and your soul manifests, and you see you truly are one with everything. Once you are present, your work is to remain in the Present. It typically takes years of practice to be able to do this.

I, like the Buddha, believe everyone has the capability to spiritually awaken. We all have a seed of a soul waiting to be nourished, waiting to grow. But, *you must desire it*. Awakening must remain at the forefront of your mind in everything you do, every moment of your life. Awakening is an active pursuit.

In a very few individuals, awakening occurs without making an active effort. However, when this happens, one typically has endured tremendous suffering, the type of extreme suffering that often can lead one to give up and die, or commit suicide. If one has the strength of spirit to endure this level of suffering, their suffering transforms them and pushes them to a higher level of consciousness and spiritual understanding. As I mentioned, this is very rare. One individual who reached a higher level of spiritual understanding due to extreme suffering was Viktor Frankl. His story and the awakening of his spiritual understanding are chronicled in his book

Man's Search for Meaning. I highly recommend it.

If you have reached a point in your life where you know that your life's work is spiritual-based, find a spiritual teacher or teaching that speaks to your soul and gives you the necessary tools to pursue your goal to awaken and become enlightened, and release your inner Buddha.

GET IN SPIRITUAL SHAPE

To keep the body in good health is a duty...otherwise we will not be able to keep our mind strong and clear.

— The Buddha

Have you ever felt too tired to make the effort to be present? Have you felt as though you didn't have the energy to overcome expressing negativity? Do you sometimes feel it is too much work to be on a spiritual path? If so, maybe you need to get in spiritual shape.

The spiritual journey is demanding. If spiritual awakening was easy, everyone would be doing it. The spiritual journey is intellectually, emotionally, physically, and instinctively challenging. Thus, it is beneficial if you don't neglect these aspects of yourself. You wouldn't run a marathon without training for it, so why wouldn't you get in spiritual shape for the most challenging endeavor of your life — *the awakening of your soul.*

I'm not suggesting you only read spiritual books, become a vegan, meditate a couple of hours a day, and do yoga each morning. But, it will help if you care for and properly maintain your intellectual, emotional, physical, and instinctive centers.

Take a moment and ask yourself, "What are the biggest obstacles regarding my spiritual journey and my ability to be present?"

Maybe you need to read more spiritual texts, which will inspire you and help you maintain focus on your spiritual journey. Maybe you need to alter your eating and sleeping habits so hunger and lack of sleep don't make you irritable and prone to expressing negativity. Maybe you are feeling lethargic and need to begin to exercise to feel more energetic. Maybe you are working too much and need to spend more quality emotional time with your spouse or loved ones. All of these can affect your desire and ability to be present.

You will find that if you neglect your intellectual, instinctive, emotional, and physical centers it will be more difficult to be present, and it will affect your ability to rise above and transform negative emotions and behaviors when they occur. You will see the benefits if you *get in spiritual shape.*

NATURE IS FOOD FOR THE SOUL

Our bodily food is changed into us, but our spiritual food changes us into itself.

—Meister Eckhart

Nature is God's art and it feeds the soul. Whenever you feel spiritually depleted and in need of nourishment, Nature is one source you can turn as it can be found everywhere. Have you ever noticed how silent and present you become in view of a glorious sunset? Or while observing butterflies and hummingbirds feeding on the nectar of flowers? Or at night, while gazing upon the constellations?

I have previously mentioned the majestic oak tree in my backyard. When I am present and sitting underneath this amazing tree, I often feel I can hear it communicating with my soul. This tree is very old and like other trees its age it has survived extreme heat and cold, plentiful rains and severe drought, lightning storms, strong winds, and hail. It has seen its limbs bend and sometimes break. Without discrimination, it serves as shelter for insects, birds, squirrels, and the occasional owl. And its enormous, sprawling canopy is a refuge from the heat during the sweltering days of summer.

This majestic oak doesn't dwell on the past nor does it worry about tomorrow. It remains present each day, accepting whatever occurs without complaining. This tree teaches me that Nature lives in the eternal Present. Nature does not judge or discriminate. *Nature is Being*.

If you are feeling the need for spiritual nourishment, spend time with Nature. You needn't look very far to find it. Nature feeds the soul. Nature is spiritual food capable of transforming you into itself.

PART III

QUESTION AND ANSWER

The more one loves the nearer he approaches to God, for God is the spirit of infinite love. And when we come into this realization of our oneness with this Infinite Spirit, then divine love so fills us that, enriching and enrapturing our own lives, from them it flows out to enrich the life of all the world.

— Ralph Waldo Trine

A SPIRITUAL CRISIS EXISTS

In your opinion, what is the current spiritual state of the U.S.?

I believe there is a significant spiritual crisis occurring in the United States. We are living in a time of great disharmony and disunity. This occurs when individuals lose sight of their true nature as spiritual Beings. We are not men and women. We are not the body. We are not the mind or thought. *We are souls.* Your body is mortal and the time it spends in the physical, material world is brief and transitory. Your soul, however, is eternal and divine.

When you believe the illusion that you are the body and mind, you begin to believe your thoughts are real and your opinions valid and correct. As a result, you become ego-driven. Your thoughts, decisions, and actions become based on the intellectual, emotional, and instinctive wants and desires of the ego.

The ego lives in fear. The fear-based mentality of the ego views its environment and the world as man versus man, me versus you, and us versus them. Hence, the ego-driven individual is selfish, fearful, and focuses chiefly on his or her self-interests and ultimate survival.

If ego-driven individuals are successful in their careers or achieve a position of power or prestige, they tend to develop a high level of self-importance and grandiosity. When this occurs, their behavior is often characterized by greed, power, and vanity. Their fear of looking bad or losing what they have gained, fuels their vanity and greed even more. These individuals will justify their arrogant and selfish actions even when their gains are at the expense and detriment of others. Hence, ego-driven individuals rarely hesitate to engage in illicit, immoral behavior under the guise of self-righteousness.

An ego-driven individual is usually void of any relative thinking, and typically views life and the world in extremes. Their speech is characterized by fear and often contains absolutes, such as: all, always, everything, every time, never, no one, and nothing. To the ego-driven individual, shades of grey do not exist. Their world is black or white, good or bad, us or them. An ego-driven person may make statements such as, "All Arabs are terrorists. Never trust anyone you don't know. Poor people are lazy. Take what is yours before someone else does. You are either for me or against me."

The soul knows we are all one through our connection with the Divine—from insects to whales, from grains of sand to stars in distant galaxies. However, because ego-driven individuals are disconnected from their souls, they often lack any real concern for the environment and its inhabitants. Instead of desiring to preserve and protect the environment, they feel the environment exists to serve their selfish needs.

The 2008 banking crisis and Bernie Madoff's Ponzi scheme are the direct result of ego-driven individuals who have lost touch with their spiritual nature. Their separation from the Infinite Spirit has caused tremendous pain and suffering to millions of individuals.

I believe it is imperative we remember our spiritual nature and gain a sense of spiritual unity. We must remember that while our country consists of many different races and religions, *ultimately we are one.*

We must love one another regardless of race, creed, or social class. In harming others, we harm ourselves. In depriving others, we deprive ourselves. We must remember we are souls connected by the Infinite Spirit. As such, there is not one person on Earth that is more important than any other person.

We must respect one another. The simplest way to do this is to treat each other as you would want to be treated. This maxim exists in all the major, world religions.

Buddhism: *Hurt not others in ways that you yourself would find hurtful.*

Christianity: *Do unto others as you would have them do unto you.*

Confucianism: *Never impose on others what you would not choose for yourself.*

Hinduism: *One should never do that to another which one regards as injurious to one's own self.*

Islam: *That which you want for yourself, seek for mankind.*

Judaism: *You shall not take vengeance or bear a grudge against your kinsfolk. Love your neighbor as yourself.*

Sikhism: *I am a stranger to no one, and no one is a stranger to me. Indeed, I am a friend to all.*

Taoism: *Regard your neighbor's gain as your own gain, and your neighbor's loss as your own loss.*

The ego resides in the intellectual center of our bodies—the mind. The soul resides in the emotional center—the heart. We must remember we are not our minds or bodies. The way to remembering you are a spiritual Being and to living a life in conscious harmony with the Infinite Spirit and Creator is to be present—to make the constant effort to live in the Eternal Now.

The Present shatters all the illusions of the ego. The Present reveals the eternal Truth. The Present will remind you that you are ultimately the loving, radiant, divine energy that is God.

When you have fully realized this, and you can no longer deny that your destiny is to live this eternal, divine Truth every waking moment of your life, the idea of loving one another unconditionally and respecting one another as you respect yourself, will move from your intellectual center into your emotional center, where the thought will translate into action.

It is not enough to talk about how wonderful the world would be if we all could just love and respect one another. We must take action. *We must love unconditionally with all our heart and soul.*

If we can love each other with the same love the Infinite Spirit has for us, a genuine concern and respect for each other and all that exists will naturally occur, and we will live in unity and conscious harmony with our Creator.

THE NATURE OF SPIRITUAL WORK

What is the basis of spiritual work?

To come to the understanding of your true na-ture as a God-realized soul. And then, to live every moment of your life based upon this realization.

How does one do this?

You remove all that is false in your life.

How do you determine what is false?

Ask yourself, "Who am I?" Any part of your answer tied to the physical world, your body, your mind, and your personality—those things are false.

I distinctly recall the birth of my son and holding him for the first time. I was very present with him. I realized in that moment that my wife and I were responsible for creating him physically, yet his soul and spirit had come from something much higher than us. I remember looking into his eyes and seeing that his body was nothing but a vehicle for a beautiful, radiant soul. And then, I saw his soul was no different from my soul. But, over time we slowly develop an identity, a personality that defines us and separates us from others. When we believe this man-made identity is real, we have lost touch with who we really are.

The purpose of spiritual work is to remember you are a soul, and we do this by living in the present moment, the eternal Now. And, if you can live every moment of your life in the Now, you will never be conflicted, angry, unhappy, dissatisfied, frustrated, unfulfilled, or have any need unmet. You will experience the mystical state of *union with the Beloved.* You will experience annihilation, yet you will feel more alive than ever before. You will experience nothingness, while at the same time, being one with everything. And, in this state of presence, if you were to wrap your arms around your body as if hugging yourself, you would feel the loving arms of God embracing you, enveloping you in divine Love. And in this moment, you will have returned home.

SPIRITUAL AWAKENING

How does one spiritually awaken?

By constantly engaging the soul. It requires tremendous effort, diligence, patience, and a little luck. Nothing is free. If you want to awaken, you must exercise your soul.

How do you exercise the soul?

By living in the Present.

Is it that simple? All you have to do is live in the Present?

Living in the Present is anything but simple. People confuse living in the Present with doing what they enjoy or living for the day. Calling in sick to work so that you can play golf with your friends is not living in the Present. Living in the Present requires you intentionally raise your level of consciousness.

I often feel like I don't have time to stop everything and be present. It seems I'm always in a hurry.

First, to be present does not require that you stop doing anything. Instead, *bring presence* to whatever activity you are engaged. Second, what are you hurrying to do? What can possibly be more important than this current moment? Nothing. This moment, right now, is all you have. Your life is *Now.*

How do you know what you know is the truth?

Do you know the Truth when you hear it? I believe you do. Man has an inherent ability to recognize Truth. Emerson said, *"The soul is the perceiver and revealer of truth."* The Truth is often accompanied by an internal, emotional understanding in the recipient, often known as "aha" moments. An "aha" moment typically occurs when you suddenly see the solution to a problem. However, it also occurs when you come into contact with the Truth. The Truth strikes a chord in you that resonates deep within, to your soul. You not only hear the Truth, but *you experience it.* You recognize it with all our heart and soul.

Yet, it is not enough to be aware of the Truth. I know people who encounter the Truth but keep searching, looking for more. Once you realize Truth, *you must live it. You must become Truth.* Otherwise, you can search forever, always learning more, but not advancing spiritually.

Is spiritual advancement our purpose for being here?

Yes. Our Creator endowed us with the ability to raise our level of consciousness, to grow as spiritual Beings. No other species on the planet has this ability. Why would God give us this incredible gift if we weren't supposed to use it? Yet, that is exactly what people do. It is no wonder the world is a big mess right now. We have lost touch with our spiritual nature. We have forgotten we are spiritual Beings whose purpose is to spiritually evolve, to grow towards the Light. Many have become *blind* to the ultimate, divine Truth.

What do you mean?

The Bible makes numerous references to the *blind*. These individuals were not without sight, physically their eyes were fine. The *blind* symbolized individuals who were *void of recognizing the spiritual Truth in the teachings of Jesus or in the word of God.* When Jesus healed the blind, he didn't restore their eyesight—He awakened their souls, which had been buried deep beneath multiple layers of false personality and ego. He made them aware of their own spiritual nature, to the spiritual Truth regarding their existence. *Jesus enabled them to see that the kingdom of God resides within. He gave them spiritual insight.*

BEING PRESENT

The focus of your teaching is being present.

There is nothing else. If you aren't present you are thinking about the past or imagining the future. Either way, you are somewhere other than being right here, right now. Shakespeare said it best when he wrote, "To be or not to be." If you are present, you are in a higher state of consciousness—*you are Being.* If you aren't present, then you basically are in a state of sleep, even though your eyes are open and you go about your day. Sometimes people have difficulty hearing this, but once they experience being present, the difference becomes very clear. You have to wake up in order to see that you were asleep.

When did you first experience being present?

As a young child, I experienced occasional moments of presence. We all do. All of the memories that you have that are incredibly vivid, those are the moments you were present. I remember the day my training wheels were removed from my bicycle, breaking my arm, having my tonsils removed, getting my first car, my wedding day, the birth of my children, and so on. In all of those moments, I was *shocked* into being present—something out of the ordinary occurred in my everyday life to bring my soul into the Now. My soul emerged and took a picture, so to speak, and my conscious memory of that moment will last forever. Yet, if you asked me what I did a week or even a few days before or after any of those events, I probably couldn't tell you anything too specific. I may have a general idea, but that's all. That's because I wasn't present to those moments. We all are shocked into being present at various moments in our lives.

More importantly, you have the ability *to make the effort to be present*. I didn't understand what this meant until I met my teacher about 20 years ago. He lived in the Now and taught me many things. He opened my eyes to a whole new world, a new way of *Being*. He helped me realize I was asleep. So, I began to remind myself in every moment of every day to be present. He also taught me the importance of transforming negative emotions. He was my teacher for 13 years.

Are you no longer in touch with him?

He passed away in early 2005. He was a lovely, gentle soul. I miss him very much. However, I can still feel his presence around me. There is much we don't understand or know about the spirit world.

Do you have a teacher now?

I have hundreds. My teachers are Jesus, Buddha, Mohammed, Plato, Socrates, Rilke, Emerson, Whitman, Lao Tzu, Marcus Aurelius, Goethe, St. John, St. Teresa, Meher Baba, Gurdjieff, I could go on and on.

However, my teachers aren't just those great Beings whose teachings show us the path to awakening. I literally find teachers all around me, all the time. My wife and children constantly teach me things. My golden retriever taught me about negativity earlier today. I have a majestic live oak in my backyard that is my teacher. Nature is an incredible teacher. When you are present, you see that everything around you has something to offer, something to teach you, but *you have to open your eyes.*

What is the biggest obstacle to being present, to living in the moment?

Your imagination. It is the basis of all your fears and desires, which are tied to the body and the ego, and keep the soul asleep. As such, your soul is literally imprisoned by the body and the ego. And, *it happens to you.* You aren't born with an ego; it is developed. And you aren't born conscious of your body; this happens over time, too. The soul becomes imprisoned, and it is up to you to free it by being present.

Why is the ego threatened of the present moment?

In the Present your soul emerges and the ego recedes into the background. Your ego has been the driving force behind all of your actions for most of your life and it wants to remain in charge. What do people in positions of power fear the most? The loss of power. It's the same with the ego. It fears a loss of power, a loss of being in control. I've seen people experience being present, and once the moment passes, their ego tries to convince them it really didn't happen, that they imagined it, or that it was actually something else. The ego wants your soul to remain its prisoner.

I've observed that I can think about being present, and then hours may go by where it doesn't occur to me. How do you develop a desire to be present?

When I first began to make efforts to be in the Present, hours and sometimes days would go by before I would think about being present again. That's because I was attempting to reverse a pattern of thinking and behavior that I had grown accustomed to my entire life. Your initial efforts to live in the Now are similar to swimming upstream. It's not easy.

One tool that can assist you in remembering to live more in the Now is to utilize *reminders*. I know people who use the ring tone on their cell phone to remind them to be present, or opening a door, walking into a room, driving in their car, things like that. You can create wonderful reminders, but they can lose their effect over time. When that happens, switch to something else. I currently wear a white reminder bracelet imprinted with "Live in Conscious Harmony" to assist me. I find it very helpful as people will also ask me about it. The moment it stops working though, I will remove it and find something else to replace it.

I find it easy to be present when I'm doing something I enjoy, but I find it very difficult to be present when I'm doing something I don't enjoy like laundry, house cleaning, or paying bills.

Those things you don't enjoy are precisely the things you need to be present to! Life is not limited to the things you enjoy. Your life is composed of every single second you are alive, every breath you take, each beat of your heart.

If you have children, do you stop being a parent when it becomes too challenging? Or, stop being a spouse during difficult times? Or, quit your job because you had a bad week at work?

Your Being is tested during the difficult times. It is not easy to be in the Now. If it were, everyone would be doing it. You must make the effort to be present all the time.

So, does the thought to be present become habitual?

Yes, but you have to remember that the thought must produce action. If you aren't making the accompanying effort, what good is it to think about it? You can think for weeks and months about starting a diet or making a big change in your life and never do it. The thought can be habitual, but it must be accompanied by effort.

One thing I have noticed is that the more you make the effort to be present, the more *you realize you must be present.* The more awake you become, the greater the need to make efforts to remain awake because going back to sleep would be the equivalent of spiritually dying long before your actual death.

FORGIVENESS & COMPASSION

Is the ego capable of forgiveness?

No. True forgiveness requires unconditional acceptance. It is based in divine Love and comes from the soul. As such, it takes Being to be able to truly forgive someone. True forgiveness has a spiritual component to it, for it is of a divine nature.

The ego pretends to forgive. Its form of forgiveness is based upon conditions that must be met, and is closer to mercy than actual forgiveness. The ego forgives, but with strings attached. In this way the ego uses forgiveness to gain power and dominance over another, and to instill fear of future repercussions. For example, the ego will state something like, "I'll forgive you this time, but if it happens again..." Hence, the ego forgives, but it never forgets. This is not true forgiveness.

Only the soul is capable of true forgiveness, for the soul, by its very nature, is divine Love and unconditional acceptance. For this reason alone, to be truly forgiven by someone is quite rare.

How can I be more compassionate towards others?

The key to being more compassionate is to engage your soul by living in the Now. When you live from your soul, you engage the Divine that exists within you. As such, you cannot help but be more compassionate, more loving, more accepting.

When you engage the soul, you see people, objects, and circumstances objectively. In the Present, all biases, opinions, and feelings dissolve away revealing the eternal Truth. It is in the Present that you see things more clearly, as God intended.

In the Now, one of the many truths you will discover is that all negativity, conflict, problems, dysfunction, wars, hatred, and violence can be broken down to one common denominator—*fear*.

Once you realize that people unknowingly act and make decisions from a place of fear, you will automatically have more compassion for them. Think about it for a moment…in the past, have you ever not felt compassionate towards someone or something that you knew was afraid?

DEALING WITH REGRET

What is the best way to deal with feelings of regret?

Regret is a negative emotion that keeps us from living in the Now. I don't know of anyone who does not have a little regret. We all have made a decision or two that, if we could do it all over again, we would make a different choice. However, regret can only exist if you are focused on the past. You cannot be regretful and be in the Present.

People tend to focus on the past and wonder *what could have been* instead of accepting who or what they are now, and instituting the necessary changes today to get their life on the right track. Individuals do this with what I commonly refer to as *if only* thinking.

"If only I had taken better care of myself, I wouldn't be having health problems. If only I had followed my dreams, I would be happy. If only I had been smarter with my money, I wouldn't be struggling financially. If only I hadn't wasted so much time, I'd be further along in my career."

Remember, all you have is the present moment. You cannot change the past, but you can change right now.

NOT EXPRESSING NEGATIVE EMOTIONS

You speak about the importance of not expressing negative emotions, and I am successful when things are going well, but I have a difficult time if someone is being mean or rude towards me. How do I not react negatively in these situations? Am I supposed to act as though it doesn't bother me?

It is natural to react negatively to bad things when they occur. However, it is important to remember that negativity is an expression of the ego, not the soul. Furthermore, if you are expressing negativity you are not living in the Now.

When someone says or does something hurtful to you, your ego will respond with negativity, and depending on the magnitude of the offense, your reaction will range anywhere between the smaller, negative emotions (annoyed, bothered, sad) to the larger, more destructive, negative emotions (anger, rage, revenge). However, you must remember *you have control over how you choose to react to every single thing that happens to you.* You can validate your ego's pain and express negativity, or you can be present and react from your soul with objectivity, acceptance, and compassion. Do not mistake the soul's reaction for complacency or passivity. It is not easy to react to hurtful situations with objectivity, acceptance, and compassion.

If someone commits a crime against you, justice should be sought, but *without you having judgment about it.* Because you do not react with negativity does not mean you don't care. It means you don't have any judgment regarding the situation. It is easy to allow the subjective ego to respond with negativity. It takes effort to be present and respond with objectivity.

DEALING WITH FEAR

I seem to make most of my decisions out of fear. I don't date because I fear being rejected. I want to start my own business, but I fear I won't make enough money. I've always paid my taxes, yet I fear being audited by the IRS! The list is endless. It's exhausting to live this way. I want to change but I don't know how.

First, it is important to recognize that your fear is not real. Fear only exists in the mind as it is based on future events occurring or not occurring. You are afraid of things that have not happened. You are making decisions and living your life in anticipation of future events.

If I say to you, "Show me the future." Can you? No. You can tell me that tomorrow is in the future, but tomorrow has no permanence. There is no guarantee of tomorrow. Tomorrow will only be real when it becomes today. To stop living in the future, you must fully understand that you only have today. Only the present moment is real.

There is a simple way to verify that fear is an illusion. Become present. Once you are present, ask yourself, "What am I afraid of now?" The answer will always be the same—nothing. When you are living in the Present, you cannot experience fear because fear does not exist in the Present. The instant you leave the Present, fear returns. The more you live in the Present, the freer you will be from making decisions based in fear.

CONSCIOUS ART

Is it possible to tell the difference between art created by the soul versus art created by the ego?

Yes. Art created from the soul is considered conscious art. It has the power to bring the viewer into the Now. Conscious art speaks to your soul and expresses Truth. Art created by the ego does not have this characteristic. It can be stylistically perfect, even considered a masterpiece, yet it does not create presence in the viewer.

Often, conscious art results from the artist having experienced higher levels of consciousness through their own efforts to spiritually evolve, and in some instances, having spiritually awakened.

The awakened soul will seek to express itself via an art form: painting, sculpting, dance, music, public speaking, theatre, architecture, poetry, writing, and the like. Examples of the soul expressing itself can be observed in the poetry and drawings of William Blake, the writings of Emanuel Swedenborg, the music of Johann Sebastian Bach, the self-portraits of Rembrandt, and the paintings of Leonardo da Vinci. In fact, some speculate that the mass appeal of *The Mona Lisa* is due to Leonardo da Vinci actually being able to capture in a painting a woman living in the Now.

It is also possible for conscious art to be created by an artist who may not be spiritually inclined. In these instances, the artist is a conduit in which the Infinite Spirit expresses itself.

If you find yourself brought into the Present when reading, viewing, or listening to a work of art, it is quite possible it is conscious, and it is providing you a glimpse into the nature of the Infinite Spirit or is expressing the divine Truth.

CHANGING ANOTHER'S CONSCIOUSNESS

Is it possible to change or affect another person's state of consciousness?

Changing or affecting another's state of consciousness happens all the time. More importantly though, is the ability *to raise another's level of consciousness.*

All your thoughts and actions, both positive and negative, consist of vibrations of energy. This energy radiates from your body and affects everyone and everything in your environment.

Have you ever been in a crowd and witnessed how one person's negative outburst can quickly spread, affecting a large group of people in a matter of seconds? Or, have you ever been around someone who was very negative, and afterward you felt as though he or she had poisoned you? Or, have you been in the company of someone who radiates joy, happiness, and love, and observed the powerful effect positive energy possesses?

Dr. Masaru Emoto conducted fascinating studies regarding the effects of positive and negative energy on water. Dr. Emoto photographed cells of water before and after the cells received positive or negative energy. The change in the cells of water was extraordinary. I highly recommend you check out the photos in his book *The Miracle of Water*. They are astounding. Considering our cells are mostly water, you can see how easily we are affected by energy. We are constantly being bombarded and affected by the energies of others, creating a change in our state of consciousness. While these changes in our state are significant, they are not as significant as the ability to literally raise another's level of consciousness.

It is possible to raise another's level of con-sciousness by being present with them. This is the most profound impact you can have on another person. While positive and negative energy changes one's state of mind, *the state of presence awakens the soul*. When you are present, you are unconditional Love. Through the power of Love, you can affect another's level of consciousness. You can be the conduit that assists in bringing them into the Now. *Unconditional Love is the greatest force that exists — it is God.*

REINCARNATION

What are your thoughts on reincarnation?

No one can prove or disprove reincarnation. However, I will say that based on observations and knowledge I have gleaned from my own experience with higher states of consciousness, the soul does not die and continues to evolve after the death of the body.

I believe upon dying, you will experience a judgment or assessment. Furthermore, *you will be your own judge.* During this judgment period, you will experience all the joy and all the pain you have caused others. Afterward, you will know the work you must do in your next incarnation to move closer towards achieving awakening and enlightenment, and breaking free of the birth-death-rebirth cycle of existence, that is, if you are on a spiritual path.

Otherwise, I believe you return to repeat life over again, but with a different body and under different circumstances.

EPILOGUE

The end of life is to be like God, and the soul following God will be like Him.

—Socrates

A MESSAGE OF THANKS

If you are reading this, I feel confident in assuming you have begun the most incredible journey you can embark upon—*the spiritual journey*. It is a journey in which you seek union with the Divine. It is a journey of awakening through God's greatest gift—*unconditional Love*.

The spiritual journey of awakening and enlightenment is ultimately a journey of recognizing the Divine that resides *within you*. When you are living in the Now, the ego's veils of ignorance that hide your divine nature, part to reveal your true nature as a radiant, spiritual Being. When you are present, you awaken to this most wonderful realization. *Hold to it and never forget it.* Whenever you have a moment of negativity, doubt, fear, or worry, take a second to be present and remember who you really are. When you are present, you not only benefit your own soul, but you also benefit the oversoul, the collective soul of mankind.

We are ultimately alone. We are born alone and we will die alone. And the spiritual work we must do, we do alone. But, we can be beacons of Light and Love and encourage each other to remain steadfast in our respective journeys.

So, thank you, fellow soul travelers. Knowing you accompany me on this wonderful, miraculous journey fills my heart with joy. You are my soul's mates.

Lastly, thank you for purchasing my book. I hope you have found value in reading it. If so, please consider subscribing to my blog Living in Conscious Harmony at www.livinginconsciousharmony.com.

Peace and Blessings,

ABOUT THE AUTHOR

Spiritual teacher, life coach, and author Sullins Stuart has studied spirituality, philosophy, and psychology for over twenty years. He holds a M.A. in counseling from St. Edward's University. In July 1995, three years into the thirteen years he spent with his own teacher, Sullins experienced a spiritual awakening that dramatically changed the direction of his life and his life's work. He has lectured across the United States and Mexico City, and his spiritual articles have been published in the Austin American Statesman. Sullins devotes his time to spiritual coaching and consulting, lecturing, writing, and furthering his spiritual growth and evolution. He lives in Austin, Texas, with his wife and two children.

To contact Sullins Stuart, subscribe to his blog, or to receive updates on lectures, events, and new releases, visit www.livinginconsciousharmony.com or www.sullinsstuart.com and click on the Contact tab.

Visit the author's website:
    www.livinginconsciousharmony.com
    www.sullinsstuart.com

Made in the USA
Monee, IL
07 July 2026